DISCOVERING CREATIVE SOLUTIONS TO EVERYDAY CHALLENGES

DUKE CORPORATE EDUCATION

DISCOVERING CREATIVE SOLUTIONS TO EVERYDAY CHALLENGES

Blair Sheppard • Michael Canning
Marla Tuchinsky • Cindy Campbell

President, Dearborn Publishing: Roy Lipner
Vice President and Publisher: Cynthia A. Zigmund
Acquisitions Editor: Jon Malysiak
Senior Project Editor: Trey Thoelcke
Interior Design: Lucy Jenkins
Cover Design: Design Solutions
Typesetting: Elizabeth Pitts

Published by Dearborn Trade Publishing
A Kaplan Professional Company

Printed in the United States of America

06 07 08 10 9 8 7 6 5 4 3 2 1

Library of Congress Cataloging-in-Publication Data

Discovering creative solutions to everyday challenges / Duke Corporate Education.
    p.   cm. — (Leading from the center)
    Includes bibliographical references and index.
    ISBN-13: 978-1-4195-1508-8
1. Creative ability in business. 2. Industrial management. I. Duke Corporate Education. II. Series.
    HD53.D57 2005
    658.4′03—dc22

                                                             2005022375

CONTENTS

ACKNOWLEDGMENTS

First and foremost, we continue to thank our clients and the many program participants around the globe. We begin our work by listening to our clients and gaining an understanding of their business challenges. Working with talented people and actively engaging in their challenges across a range of industries and geographies has afforded us the opportunity to learn and develop an informed point of view on these topics. We thank our clients for trusting in our approach and making us part of their teams. They have shared their experiences and have discussed at length the skills, tools, and mind-sets covered in this book that have deepened our knowledge and insight.

We also are fortunate to have an extensive network of faculty, coaches, facilitators, and partners who believe in our mission and have opted to join in our adventure. Together, we have delivered programs in 37 different countries since we formed Duke CE in July 2000. We absolutely could not have accomplished what we have and learned what we did without their collaboration.

Many thanks to all of those on the Dearborn team, who continue to provide valuable feedback and guide us each step of the way. Their assistance and patience is much appreciated.

Jan Tuchinsky has been kind enough to find time to sit and chat with us on multiple occasions, sharing her experiences and stories of what life is really like for those managers in the middle of organizations, large and small. She has been a great source of insight and ideas whenever we needed some help with our own "creative spark." We hope she has enjoyed the process as well.

On many occasions we've approached Bill Lahti (often with short turnaround timelines) and asked him to read through our manuscripts. He's always been happy to help and his feedback has provided great insight.

We have been fortunate to have had the writing, research, and editing assistance of Elizabeth Brack for several of our books, and

Betsy has again been a key part of the team in bringing this work to completion. Her help and support have been immeasurable.

Although often working with vague instructions, Ryan Stevens helped to capture our methods and processes in the graphical images included within the book. As usual, he did a wonderful job.

As always, we could not have accomplished this without the guidance and assistance of our CEO, Blair Sheppard. He supported this initiative from the outset, and more importantly, always made time to review our output and guide our thinking. His assistance is without measure. We could not have done it without him.

We've drawn upon the insight, experience, and expertise from numerous colleagues here at Duke CE. We hope that the content of this book stimulates your thinking and improves your ability to develop and pursue innovative solutions to the challenges you face.

The *Discovering Creative Solutions to Everyday Challenges* team: Michael Canning, Marla Tuchinsky, and Cindy Campbell.

INTRODUCTION

In the past 30 years, they have been repeatedly laid off, outsourced, replaced by information technology applications, and insulted with such derogatory names as "the cement layer." Their bosses accused them of distorting and disrupting communication in their organizations, and their subordinates accused them of thwarting the subordinates' autonomy and empowerment. Who are "they"? Middle managers, those managing in the middle of the organization.

With such treatment, you might think that middle managers are villainous evildoers who sabotage companies, or obstructionist bureaucrats who stand in the way of real work getting done. However, the reality is just the opposite. When performed well, the middle manager role is critical in organizations.

Although over the past several decades the value and stature of middle managers has seen both high and low points, we at Duke Corporate Education believe that managing in the center of the organization has always been both critically important and personally demanding. As one would expect, the essence of the role—the required mind-set and skill set—has continued to change over time. The need to update each of these dimensions is driven by periodic shifts in such underlying forces as marketplace dynamics, technology, organizational structure, and employee expectations. Now and then, these forces converge to create an inflection point that calls for a "step change" in how organizations are governed; this has particular implications for those managing in the center.

In the *Leading from the Center* series, we examine some of these primary causes that are shaping what it means to successfully lead from the center in the modern organization. We outline the emerging imperative for middle management in an organization as well as the mind-set, knowledge, and skills required to successfully navigate through the most prevalent challenges that lie ahead.

THE NEW CENTER

There are four powerful and pervasive trends affecting the role that managers in the center of an organization are being asked to assume. These trends—information technology, industry convergence, globalization, and regulations—connect directly to the challenges these managers are facing.

Compared to twenty or thirty years ago, *information technology* has escalated the amount, speed, and availability of data to the point that it has changed the way we work and live. Access to information has shifted more power to our customers and suppliers. They not only have more information, but are directly involved in and interacting with the various processes along the value chain. On a personal level, we now find ourselves connected to other people all the time; cell phones, pagers, BlackBerrys, and PDAs all reinforce the 24/7 culture. The transition from work week to weekend and back is less distinct. These micro-transitions happen all day, every day because many of us remain connected all the time.

Industries previously seen as separate are now seeing multiple points of *convergence.* Think about how digital technology has led to a convergence of sound, image, text, computing, and communications. Longstanding industry boundaries and parameters are gone (e.g., cable television companies are in the phone business, electronics companies sell music), and along with them, the basis and nature of competition. The boundaries are blurred. It's clear that new possibilities, opportunities, and directions exist, but it isn't always clear what managers should do. Managers will have to be prepared to adapt; their role is to observe, learn from experience, and set direction dynamically. Layered on top of this is the need to manage a more complex set of relationships—cooperating on Monday, competing on Tuesday, and partnering on Wednesday.

Globalization means that assets are now distributed and configured around the world to serve customers and gain competitive advantage. Even companies that consider themselves local interact with global organizations. There is more reliance on fast-developing regional centers of expertise. For example, computer programming in India and manufacturing in China. This means that middle managers are interacting with and coordinating the efforts of people who live in different cultures, and may be awake while their managers are asleep. The notion of a workday has changed as the work straddles time zones. The nature of leading has changed as it becomes more common to partner with vendors and work in virtual teams across regions.

The first three forces are causing shifts in the fourth—the *regulatory environment*. Many industries are experiencing more regulation, while a few others are experiencing less. In some arenas now experiencing more regulation, there is also a drive for more accountability. Demand for more accountability leads to a greater desire to clarify boundaries and roles. Yet there is more ambiguity as to what the rules are and how best to operationalize them. Consider how, in the wake of Sarbanes-Oxley legislation, U.S. companies and their accountants continue to sort through the new requirements, while rail companies in Britain are negotiating which company is responsible for maintaining what stretch of tracks. Middle managers sit where regulations get implemented and are a critical force in shaping how companies respond to the shifts in the environment.

All of these changes have implications for those managing at the center of organizations. No small group at the top can have the entire picture because the environment has more of everything: more information and connectivity, a faster pace, a dynamic competitive space, greater geographic reach, better informed and connected customers and suppliers, and shifting legal rules of the game. No small group can process the implications, make thoughtful decisions, and disseminate clear action steps. The top of the organization needs those in the center to help make sense of the dynamic environment. The connection between strategy development and strategy execution becomes less linear and more interdependent and, therefore, managers in the center become pivotal actors.

As we said earlier, the notion of the middle of an organization typically conjures up a vertical image depicting managers in the center of a hierarchy. This mental image carries with it a perception of those managers as gatekeepers—controlling the pace at which information or resources flow down or up. It appears to be simple and linear.

However, as many of you are no doubt experiencing, you now find yourselves navigating in a matrix, and as a node in a network or

FIGURE I.1 In the Center of the Action

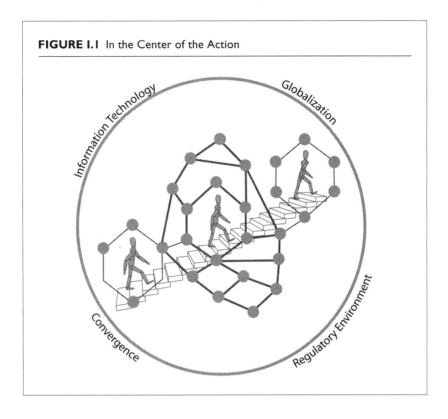

multiple networks. As depicted in Figure I.1, this new view of the center conjures up images of centrality, integration, connection, and catalyst. *You are in the center of the action, not the middle of a hierarchy.* When you overlay this connected view on the traditional vertical notion, it produces some interesting tensions, trade offs, and opportunities. Your formal authority runs vertically, but your real power to achieve results stems from your ability to work across all levels and boundaries.

IF YOU ARE LEADING FROM THE CENTER

If you are a manager in the center today, you have many hats to wear, more balls to juggle, and fewer certainties in your work environment. You have to be adaptive yet provide continuity in your leadership. You need to simultaneously translate strategy, influence and collaborate, lead teams, coach and motivate, support innovation, and own the systems and processes—all in the service of getting results. Those in the center need more courage than ever. You are the conscience of your organization, carrying forth the values, and at the same time building today's and tomorrow's business success.

Strategy Translator

As a strategy translator, you must first understand the corporate strategy and determine what parts of it your group can best support. Next, you must translate it into an action plan for your group, making sure it aligns well to the overall strategy. You'll need to consider which projects are essential stepping stones and which are needed in their own right, and establish some priorities or guiding goals. You must then communicate the details of the plan and priorities, and create momentum around them. As your team implements, you'll need to involve not only your people but to also collaborate and coordinate with others, including peers, customers, and other units. Instead of directing a one-way downward flow of information, you must translate upward as well and act as a conduit for strategic feedback to the executives above.

Influencer and Collaborator for Results

Middle managers must learn how to make things happen by influencing, integrating, and collaborating across the boundaries of the organization. As a manager, instead of focusing exclusively on your piece, you have to look outside of your own group to develop a network of supporting relationships. Rather than issuing commands and asserting power based on your position, you have to use other tactics to gain agreement and make things happen.

Leader of Teams

Teams have become a one-size-fits-all solution for organizing work in today's economy—virtual teams, project teams, product teams, and function-specific teams—and can be either the blessing or the bane of many companies. Your role as a manager includes understanding the challenges of teams and facilitating their development so that they can be effective more quickly. You have to align the team's energy and talents in a way that will deliver the desired results. You are responsible for creating an environment that will help this group of people work well together to achieve today's objectives and to develop the skills needed to take on future goals.

Coach and Motivator

Many organizations are well positioned to execute their strategies in yesterday's environment, they are moderately able to meet their current needs, and often they are not thinking about how to position themselves for the future. From the center of the organization, middle managers assume much of the responsibility for their people. They create an environment to attract and retain good employees, coach them to do their current jobs better, and bear primary responsibility for developing others. As a manager, you must figure out how to build the next level of capability, protect existing people, connect their aspirations to opportunities for development, and make work more enjoyable. You need to provide regular feedback—both positive and redirecting—and build strong relationships with those who surround you. If done well, your departments will be more efficient and your employees will be better equipped to become leaders in their own right.

Intrapreneur/Innovator

Enabling and supporting an innovative approach within your company will foster the strategic direction of the future. To effectively sponsor innovation, you need to create the context for your people, foster a climate that supports innovative efforts, and actively sponsor the ideas of the future. You have to *be* innovative and *lead* the innovative efforts of others. Innovation is most often associated with new-product development, but innovative approaches also are needed in developing new services or solving internal system and process problems. As a manager, you use your influence and relationships to find the root cause of problems, and the resources to make change happen.

Owner of Systems and Processes

You need to understand that part of your role is to take ownership for architecting new systems and processes. You will have to shift your thinking from living within existing systems and processes to making sure that those systems and processes work well: Do the systems and processes support or get in the way of progress? One of the mistakes we have made in the past is not holding managers accountable for their role in architecting the next generation of systems and processes. As a manager, you must perform harsh audits of existing systems, and understand when to tear down what may have been left in place from a past strategy. You need to assess what is no longer relevant and/or is no longer working. Part of your responsibility is to think about and decide whether to re-engineer or remove existing systems.

SHIFTS IN MIND-SET NEEDED FOR THE FUTURE

Managers must simultaneously get results today and build for the future. As a product of the dynamic and complex world in which we do business, managers today are encountering both greater complexity to their existing challenges and new challenges that have no "tried and true" solutions. Applying existing methods or solutions in the same way that you've done in the past will no longer work. These challenges will require new approaches, new mind-sets, and in many cases novel solutions.

New opportunities—client ideas, a changing industry, market moves, new problems, emerging technology, shifting strategy—will develop and wane. You must decide which opportunities or problems to spend time on. Many will include unique situations that you haven't seen before, and for which the typical solutions that you've used in the past will not work to get the results you need. You'll need to experiment and build new solutions.

Discovering creative solutions will take more than generating new ideas—you will have to follow through and develop these new ideas into solutions that work. In this book, we propose that being creative and innovative isn't magic, and it's not the job of a few; it's a process and technique that you can learn, and one that is a shared responsibility across the organization.

As a manager, you have a dual challenge of doing and leading—of being actively engaged in innovative process efforts, while also managing the logistics and resources to support others' efforts. Ultimately, you need to be an architect for the future, building a culture that supports and fosters an innovative process approach. You will learn how to develop and meet each of these facets of your role through the tips and techniques we offer.

CHAPTER ONE

THE CHALLENGE OF DISCOVERING CREATIVE SOLUTIONS

IN THIS CHAPTER

It Takes More Than Ideas ■ Why Is It Important? ■
Lead the Process, Build the Culture ■ Basic Principles

Archimedes is considered one of the greatest mathematicians of all time, and is credited with several innovative discoveries. Legend has it that one day "the wise one" climbed into his bathtub and noticed that the amount of water that overflowed the tub was directly proportional to the amount of his body that was submerged beneath the water. Supposedly, he was so excited that he ran naked through the streets of Syracuse shouting, "*Eureka! Eureka!*" (In Greek that means "I found it! I found it!") He continued experimenting, and eventually crafted several rules that are still recognized today correlating weight, volume, and associated buoyancy; basically, these principles explain how submarines can submerge and rise to the surface. We consider them common knowledge today, but they were novel concepts in Archimedes's time.

IT TAKES MORE THAN IDEAS

That spark of inspiration . . .
The "lightbulb" moment . . .
A wacky idea that *just* might work . . .
And, of course, the "Eureka!" shout . . .

All of the above characterize how we typically view creative problem solving—a flash of insight and you have the answer. However, that's not usually how we find lasting approaches. What *does* it take to come up with creative solutions to common problems? How can you tap into your strengths and leverage other people's talents to find innovative ways of handling these challenges?

It takes an open mind. At a basic level, discovery can come from a few distinct sources: looking at something in a new way, changing an established method, or putting ordinary things together in a new or different way. In each of these three cases, you have to recognize that the status quo isn't the only path. If you aren't actively seeking, observing, and open to looking at opportunities through a new lens, you can't make a discovery.

Many "new" products and services aren't new; they're just new combinations. A series of 1980s commercials for a popular candy bar showed people in various situations—at the movies or just walking along—who somehow ran into one another. One was eating a chocolate bar, while the other was eating peanut butter from a jar—admittedly a bit odd, but it's a commercial. Through some bizarre twist of fate, one managed to drop his chocolate into the other's jar of peanut butter. They then exclaim, "Hey! You got your chocolate in my peanut butter!" and "You got your peanut butter in my chocolate!" And thus, we are led to believe, this is how the Reese's Peanut Butter Cup was first created.

When you discover a solution that works, occasionally it presents itself in a flash of brilliance (chocolate and peanut butter taste good together!), without a lot of effort on your part, or the solution may appear as the result of a lucky mistake. More often, however, creative solutions are the product of a lot of discipline and hard work by a broad assortment of talented people. For example, scientists and researchers in pharmaceutical companies often test 5,000 to 10,000 different compounds (molecules or substances) before finding one that actually will become an approved drug. Successfully bringing that one new drug to the public has an average cost of nearly $900 million and takes 10 to 12 years. By the time the drug becomes commercially available, the process has required the talent, knowledge, and skill of thousands of people beyond the scientists in the lab—from numerous clinical trials with test patients, to regulatory approval, to packaging, to marketing, and, finally, to the pharmacy. All that work requires seeing a possibility and experimenting from there.

It's more than new stuff or big ideas. Being innovative is also more than just flashy new products and inventions. Discovering creative solutions is about taking advantage of the variety of opportunities that present themselves—to solve problems, to improve processes, to incorporate new technologies, or to extend what already exists—whether a process, product, or service—in a way that produces a solution to the problems or opportunities you are facing. It could be an incremental improvement to an existing product, process, or system. It may simply be a clever response to a new opportunity that you are exploring for the first time.

It may be a novel solution to a known problem or opportunity. The head of a small, family-owned trucking business tackled the decades-old problem of air pressure fluctuations in big-rig tires. Improper air pressure affects fuel efficiency, safety, and the lifespan of tires. John Becker and his team at Trans Technologies invented a rotary air chamber that attaches to the wheels of semi trucks and trailers. This device regulates air pressure in the tire by removing or adding air to keep tires at a safe driving pressure throughout a long haul. Becker noted: "There are six other systems that inject air into tires, but the problem is if you start here (Georgia) with 100 pounds of pressure and drive to Arizona, the air pressure rises. We're the only people in the world who have figured out how to let air *out* of the tire." (Phillips, 2005)

Being innovative also may include applying a known solution in a new way. Leeches, commonly used in the 1800s to treat a variety of illnesses, fell out of favor until recently when reconstructive and cosmetic surgeons began to use them to restore blood circulation in patients. The leeches help prevent a condition where blood pools in damaged tissue. If the blood buildup can't be removed quickly, the blood will coagulate and form clots that can clog arteries, thus causing tissue to die. Although they're inexpensive, there are some downsides. Some patients are a bit squeamish, leeches aren't sterile, and the nurses don't like working with them. So, at least one manufacturer has designed a mechanical (and less slimy) version of this ancient remedy.

"I'd like to remind you again, Winfield, that daydreaming is only a part of the creative process."

Innovation is for everyone. The words *creative* or *innovative* may not be the first words that come to mind when asked to describe your own talents and strengths. You might define your strengths primarily in terms of other capabilities, such as strategic visioning, team building, technical expertise, or project management—those capabilities you consider very critical to getting results. Maybe you're not even sure that you can be creative, or that it's important.

Within many organizations, perhaps your own, people may tend to link the role of being creative or innovative only with certain areas, such as R&D or product development. That may have been the norm in the past; however, in today's workplace, developing creative solutions must be distributed across the whole organization. Relying on the talents of a few people to produce "Eureka!" moments will not develop the sustainable solutions that you need. Those few "creative types" can't have all the answers, particularly to improving processes in your area, and they can't do it alone. Finding sustainable solutions to the complex problems and opportunities facing you today will require the *collective* creativity, talents, knowledge, and hard work of many people across the organization and beyond.

It's not magic; it's a process. How can you best address the opportunities confronting you? Discovering creative solutions is accomplished through an innovation process that begins with identifying a problem or an opportunity that is worth pursuing—an opportunity whose solution will bring real value—and then taking that opportunity to the next level.

It often begins with an opportunity that has direct meaning for you; if an issue or problem interests you, your creativity is more likely to begin sparking. Dr. Bob Lyons, recipient of a 2004 Manning Innovation Award for his work in developing a lifesaving wristband for children, called the "Safety Turtle," said in an interview that he began thinking about developing this type of product when friends almost lost a child in a pool accident. Understanding how quickly children can disappear from sight and maneuver around devices designed to keep them *out* of the pool, Dr. Lyons instead focused on a way to know quickly that kids were in trouble. He began experimenting and collaborating on this wireless device that triggers an immediate remote alarm when immersed in water—a swimming pool, a lake, or simply a bathtub. Designed for children, it's also been adapted to protect others at risk, such as pets, senior citizens, and the disabled. (Manning, 2004)

In other cases, it's someone you interact with closely who notices the opportunity. Dr. James Hannoosh, creator of the "Raising Cane," a bottom-weighted walking stick that is self-righting when dropped or knocked over, credits his father with this walking stick idea. His parents had been injured in an automobile accident, and his mother required the use of a cane during recovery—which she kept dropping and his father kept retrieving. Observing his father's frustration inspired Hannoosh to invent. (Hannoosh, 2005)

In both cases, the opportunity for improvement presented itself as part of their everyday lives, and both individuals took the opportunity to the next level. Others had probably noted these problems before, or even thought about how they could be solved, but that's where it ended. Lyons and Hannoosh were willing to put in the time and effort to think more deeply, experiment, and bring their solutions to fruition.

Similarly, opportunities originate from many sources in your work environment, and they often are connected to a desire to get better results:

- Make a task easier, faster, or more fun.
- Add missing features to products and services.
- Attract a broader customer base.
- Solve a problem.
- Save money.

Discovering solutions requires *both* generating new ideas and then applying them in a useful way: new methods, customs, devices, approaches, combinations, or changes in a process. New ideas are important, but generating ideas is typically not the problem. There are more than enough ideas to go around. Truly creative solutions require experimenting with the ideas, making unique connections, and—when you eventually find the combination that works—actually implementing it. Too many times, people get caught up in the ideas and never manage to get to the most critical part of the process—implementing a solution that works.

Creative solutions emerge through hard work and through a multistage process. As a manager, you may shepherd an idea through the initial conception, a battery of experiments and prototypes, and finally to a widely-used final form. Perhaps you may be a sponsor for someone else leading a project. Either way, you have to be open to surprises.

WHY IS IT IMPORTANT?

Although those at the top may develop strategic directions and issue general directives, it is up to you to adapt them to fit the local situation and get results. In many cases, you will be entering new territory in which there are no given or standard ways of operating. There may be no one around who has had this particular problem before. There will, instead, be many unknowns and new territory to explore. You will encounter roadblocks that you didn't anticipate—in fact, that you couldn't have anticipated because the world is changing so rapidly. These roadblocks will require creative approaches and new techniques. You need to be able to react quickly but responsibly, and it needs to happen at all levels.

Good ideas can come from anyone. For example, a company had a group of people who painted labels on the company's products. The products were basically large metal tubes of different diameters. The company was going through a tough business cycle, and needed to find ways to cut costs. This painting group was a target; they had, for example, three people who just managed the spray paint inventory. To make matters worse, the team itself had to find ways to replace themselves; that is, do the same work with fewer people. A colleague of ours acted as a consultant to the group. Different subsets met to brainstorm options. In one of these meetings, a young guy sat staring at his Coke can. He was newly hired, and hesitant to speak, but finally pointed to the can and asked the group, "how do they paint these?" One of the more senior members saw the possibility, too, and said that his brother-in-law worked for Coke and he could find out. The result? They ordered a customized version of the aluminum can painter, saving the company hundreds of thousands of dollars. The subteam did lose their jobs painting tubes, but the company was so impressed with their solution that management found all of them other jobs in another division.

Opportunities can come from multiple sources as well. Consider a restaurant and its reliance on its suppliers. Let's say a shipment of much-anticipated soft-shell crab doesn't come in on time. Restaurant regulars are eagerly anticipating the chef's unique treatment of the shellfish. They made reservations weeks in advance, knowing the window of opportunity for this succulent crab was small. Important business dinners are to take place around this special event. The chef must come up with a way to solve the problem, save face, and provide his diners with an equally exciting and memorable eating experience—without the "star" ingredient. How he solves the problem will impact his future interactions with his regulars, so his solution needs to be creative, quick, and tasty.

The cycle time between ideas and solutions is getting shorter. Managers' abilities to be innovative—to take opportunities and ideas to the next level to solutions that work—is a huge source of competitive advantage for companies. Having an insight isn't enough; it's what you *do* with that insight that will make the difference.

LEAD THE PROCESS, BUILD THE CULTURE

As managers, you have a dual challenge—to address immediate problems or opportunities and to build a culture to support your efforts. In addressing your own opportunities, you need a different approach, a creative or innovative process approach that can enable you to generate a set of ideas, to experiment, and to find valuable sustainable solutions. You also need to build the approach into the culture, into the way you and your team think about your jobs, and into the way you look at the world. Where will the next good idea come from, and how will your team turn that idea into something valuable?

Answers won't appear magically (from the top or elsewhere) and will require work. You should be a catalyst for building solutions—able to identify the right opportunities to pursue, to deeply understand and reframe the issues, to cross boundaries, and to bring the right people together in generating ideas and experimenting, so that you can generate solutions and results that matter.

You also need to manage the implementation of these creative solutions. You need to foster an environment that inspires others to be creative and to apply their talents to a range of issues over time, recognizing that creative solutions can and should occur throughout all areas of the company and not be delegated to a few. Your role is to apply innovative approaches and lead others in doing so as well.

Creating solutions in a company requires a variety of capabilities, including people who can generate new ideas and generate novel, thoughtful approaches to existing or potential challenges and opportunities, as well as people who are adept at experimenting with those ideas in order to develop workable solutions. You can't do this alone. You need to collaborate with others, to get them excited and energized about the possibilities, and you need to get them increasingly engaged in the process as you experiment and get closer to finding solutions.

The best solution isn't one that considers only the implications and benefits for your group or team. You will generate the best results by engaging a diverse group of people across multiple boundaries who can understand the interdependencies, connections, and long-term implications for the entire organization. You need a variety of people not only because some are good at generating ideas or at testing and experimenting, but because only as a group can you envision the potential effect that successful solutions could have. The more complex the project, the more critical it is for you to "connect the dots" between what you're trying to do and potential unintended consequences. A diverse team helps you understand how a solution in one area may mean trouble for another, and takes steps to avoid these problems.

When Amazon.com began its business in 1995, its founder, Jeff Bezos, knew that package delivery would be a critical component of the fledgling company's success or failure. UPS was able to offer the company reliable delivery and a massive infrastructure of ground, air, and international shipping channels. Employees at both companies were able to create a plan to meet the growing demand for Amazon.com products and positive customer experiences. One creative solution for customer service inquiries involved integrating the UPS Online Tracking tool into Amazon.com's Web site to allow customers to quickly access information about their shipment. This "creative solution" accomplished several goals, including increasing customer satisfaction and decreasing costs for the company by cutting down on customer contacts.

Jointly building creative solutions extended into Amazon.com's tenth anniversary celebration. To highlight its appreciation of customers, the company teamed up with UPS for a special ten-day series of "surprise deliveries." From July 6–16, 2005, the company planned special, celebrity deliveries of Amazon.com goods across the country. As noted in the company's press release: "Customers might open their doors to find . . . Moby hand-delivering his recently released CD 'Hotel,' or Jason Alexander with a 'Seinfeld' DVD." (UPS, 2005) Rather than celebrate their decade of business with a traditional party, the company developed this creative approach to reward its customers as well as to highlight its important business relationship with UPS.

BASIC PRINCIPLES

You should create an environment where collaboration and experimentation is the norm and well supported, an environment that will enable the connection of ideas to challenges. As you begin the process, keep the following six guiding ideas in mind that we believe will help you be successful in navigating some of the pitfalls.

1. *Innovation requires focus.* Without focus, creative ideas either never make it to solutions, or they become solutions that don't matter. They may just remain interesting ideas that never get refined or developed; solutions to problems that don't matter will never become implemented or institutionalized. Neither one is useful. Managers have to be clear what results they are trying to achieve and ensure that they are focusing on the most important objectives.

2. *Get comfortable with "fuzzy logic."* You will have to move forward and make decisions, even with unknowns, uncertainties, and incomplete information. Use the diverse skills, knowledge, and talents of those on your team and across your network to help guide you in placing your bets. Learn as you go, but you have to get started.

3. *Increment your way to solutions.* Develop solutions step by step and grow your experiments, resources, and commitments in increments. Looking back at the beginnings of their efforts, people often report that if they had known just *how* complex or hard it would be, or if they had realized everything that

would be involved in terms of time or resources, they might
never have gotten started. Realize that sunk costs are an important part of innovation; people think, "We've come this
far; we might as well see it through or all that work we've done
will have been for nothing." Growing a project incrementally
helps build commitment. Borrow resources as you go, get permission as you go, and move out from under the radar in
stages.

4. *Expect to be under-resourced.* Don't let that stop you from getting
   started. You will have to get comfortable with scarcity and be
   prepared to work the system to borrow, beg, or take what you
   need to enable a feasible experiment. Any valuable idea will
   be harder and take more effort than you initially believed.
   Stay in the game by getting increasing commitments as you
   go. As you have some success, it will become easier to get resources.

5. *Be a student and a connector.* Remain curious and continue to
   learn. Gain deeper knowledge in your area of expertise but
   also extend your curiosity and learning into areas that are less
   familiar. Creativity often happens from being steeped deeply
   in a subject or exploring in the margins and boundaries between functions. Learn more and see if you can apply what
   you learn to what you already know. Connect data or knowledge from different domains.

6. *Don't do it for the glory.* You won't succeed if you have to own
   the solution personally or receive the credit and recognition
   for creating it. Include others and make everyone a part of
   the success; you'll ultimately need their ideas and support to
   make it happen. You have to trust that the people who matter
   will know and recognize your contribution.

CHAPTER TWO

TAKING THE FIRST STEP

IN THIS CHAPTER

The Process of Innovation ■ A Challenge at
Each Step ■ Common Pitfalls

A common misperception about innovation is that all you need
to do is to have that one great insight. Innovation is not quite a case
of "Eureka! I've innovated!" It involves not just an insight, but working through how to effectively *apply* that insight. It involves a process
of transforming the "Aha!" into a sustainable solution, product, or
process.

At its core, innovation is like scientific research. You have a problem to solve, or you're curious about something, or you want to improve the way that things are done. You gather information, search
broadly, explore options, and then, *click*, something falls into place.
You understand a piece of it. You begin to experiment, to test what
you think you understood, to see if there's a practical way to use it,
to find an efficient process to get a repeatable result. After you are
confident in your initial work, you share your discovery more broadly
and let others build on your initial "find."

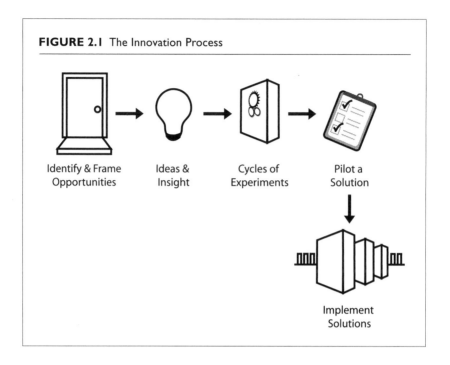

FIGURE 2.1 The Innovation Process

Identify & Frame Opportunities

Ideas & Insight

Cycles of Experiments

Pilot a Solution

Implement Solutions

THE PROCESS OF INNOVATION

"Mistakes, obviously, show us what needs improving.
Without mistakes, how would we know what we had to work on?"
Peter McWilliams, *Life 101*

In short, there is a process to creating solutions that works at multiple levels. It is an approach that works to develop large-scale solutions, such as new products or improved processes, and also can be used to develop creative solutions to everyday problems. A typical innovation process flows something like the example depicted in Figure 2.1. Between each step of the process, there are some decisions to make: who to involve, how to get resources, and whether to continue to the next step. There are five steps to follow:

1. Identify and frame the various opportunities that exist and decide which opportunity is worth pursuing.
2. Generate ideas and insight on how to approach the opportunity and decide which idea is the best bet.

3. Work through multiple iterations of experiments and proto-types, adjusting, learning, and adapting as you go.
4. Pilot (do a trial run of) viable solutions with others to learn more.
5. Implement and institutionalize solutions.

As an example of the process, consider how one Duke CE team created a new learning experience for a client. The audience was se-nior executives, an audience who sometimes can be resistant to in-struction, because they are supposed to be experts with decades of experience. So what could we possibly have to tell them that they didn't already know? To reach and teach these folks, we learned we need to take them out of their normal roles and put them in parallel situations—where they *aren't* the experts. So, we create an elaborate and realistic (but unfamiliar) setting, using actors, props, audiovisual pieces and experts from another occupation or setting. Then, we im-merse the executives in that other profession—for example, archeol-ogy or investigative journalism—to give them a new situation and set of tasks in which to practice skills/behaviors they'll need for their own jobs—e.g. interview skills, weighing data, or crafting a pointed message.

Identify the Opportunity	An energy client had asked us to help prepare its executives to execute their strategy in their changing industry. We saw this as an opportunity to immerse the executives in a scenario that forced them to consider how they might respond as an industry under attack. Participants would need to understand deeply the interplay between corporations, government, interest groups, and the press.

Ideas and Insight	After much brainstorming, we decided to remove them from their own industry and engage them in a completely different context. We contacted a client in the pharmaceutical industry who was happy to help us develop something around his industry. Although different businesses, both energy and pharma were highly regulated and under scrutiny from many directions. We hoped that learning about pharma could offer insights to our energy execs.
Cycles of Experiments	Creating this experience required us to work closely with several different groups—our design team, the energy client, our pharma contact, a cast of actors—and develop a script, set of materials, and players who would bring the situation to life. Three weeks later, our pharma contact had to withdraw. Now without our key knowledge resource, the team regrouped and went back to the basics: What were the key outcomes and critical elements of the experience? How else might we get there? After rejecting many options (including nuclear energy, asbestos, genetically modified foods) we settled on tobacco. We had a topic, but no industry insider to help guide us, and less time to design. Welcome to the innovation process! One member of our team plunged into research mode, and became our expert. We worked through several iterations of materials, continually checking that what we were building would match the participants' needs.

Pilot a Solution	Once the team created the initial story and flow for how the events would unfold, we tested our "industry under attack" with a group of mock participants. They acted as if they were the energy executives who we were now having be tobacco executives, and we went through the exercises of having their industry attacked, having to answer to a press corps waving microphones, consulting with their legal experts and line people, and engaging in all the other actions they'd need to take.
Implement Solutions	Given the success of the pilot, we then included this experience as a part of the program design. The energy executives made the connections between the mock situation and real work issues. The next challenge in the process was to figure out how to take this solution and scale it to a global audience.

Looking at the general process, keep a few things in mind. First, note that usually there is no set timescale. A few innovative solutions may happen quickly—in a couple of days or weeks—and remain sustainable over a long period of time. Liquid Paper is one such solution. In 1956, Bette Nesmith Graham, a secretary and aspiring artist in Dallas, Texas, sought a better way to fix typing errors. Her knowledge of paint came in handy, and she quickly created a correction fluid that kept her boss from noticing her errors. Word spread; soon she was making batches for friends and coworkers. She called the fluid "Mistake Out" and later started the company by the same name, which became the Liquid Paper Corporation. The product has moved from one simple idea and solution to becoming an everyday product found in homes and offices. (Bellis, 2005)

Ideas may come quickly, experiments may go smoothly, the organizational players may support the effort, and life is happy. However,

Liquid Paper is more the exception than the norm. In most cases, the process takes longer. It may take a significant time commitment to develop and prototype practical and sustainable solutions.

Second, experimenting is critical to finding a solution. Persistence is often just as critical. It took Edison's labs several *thousand* attempts before they had a reliable, long-life lightbulb. Nobel Laureate T.S. Eliot wrote and edited pieces from 50 drafts to make the final poem, "The Waste Land." (MacLeod, 2005) If you and your team want to innovate, then you need to be willing to try, fail, and try again. Experimentation will require many attempts. It is rare that someone's insight yields the perfect application on the first try.

Finally, it's worth thinking about what type of assistance you might need at different phases and how you will recruit and engage others in your process. Those who can help experiment may not be those who can pilot the solution, for example. How do you share enough of your vision to get others to join in with their resources and support? Homer Hickam's bestselling memoir *Rocket Boys* (later adapted for the film *October Sky*) provides a good example of gradually engaging more and more people in a quest that begins as a very personal one. Hickam describes his childhood in the small mining town of Coalwood, West Virginia, and his dream to join the space race after watching Sputnik streak across the sky in 1957. His idea of building rockets starts as simply his own dream, with little help or resources. First, he convinces some friends to join in. The "Rocket Boys" initially see their rocket building as something fun to do in an otherwise boring town, but then, it becomes a challenge to defy their parents' wishes and to exceed the town's expectations. Over time, more people quietly become engaged in their project—his mom covers some of their testing mishaps, a local man helps with some metalwork, another offers some supplies. Eventually, many people in the town get involved, and the project's success becomes a source of shared civic pride for the townspeople. (Hickam, 1998)

A CHALLENGE AT EACH STEP

Throughout the various phases of the process, there are best practices and predictable difficulties. In the following chapters, we'll discuss these challenges and offer some advice on how you might best approach them.

Challenge #1: Seeing opportunities to innovate. How do you know what needs a creative solution? Sometimes you find a problem needing a solution, or recognize when a solution you have matches a problem, or simply sense when there is a ripe opportunity. You realize that you can take what you already know and apply it in a new way.

Challenge #2: Gaining insight, ideas, and resources. How do you get started? First, you need to get both broad and deep knowledge about the problem or situation. Tap into your own team and people networks; effectively, this helps you expand your experience and knowledge base, both of which can help you find creative ideas that lead to an eventual innovation. Then, find enough resources—ask for, quietly borrow, and even more quietly appropriate what you need to get started.

Challenge #3: Placing good bets. So many ideas, so few resources, so little time to pursue them all. You need to place a bet on a subset of the ideas you have. Which ones have the most promise— which are likely to succeed, likely to address a real issue, or likely to provide a good return on investment?

Challenge #4: Working toward a solution you can implement. Innovation takes work. You need to experiment or test your idea, learn from the test, adjust, and try again. Each round helps you get to a solution you can really use, or to get enough data to know if you should stop.

Challenge #5: Letting go so it can grow. A great paradox of innovation in organizations is that you need to nurture innovations carefully so they can survive long enough to catch on, then quickly relinquish control and let others adopt it as their own. Innovators and sponsors need to know when to let go, so their project can gain momentum and grow.

This last challenge is particularly paradoxical yet common: how to provide enough support yet not smother or impede growth. Like managing a team, it's about setting a direction and providing resources, yet not micromanaging and controlling your people.

COMMON PITFALLS

Transforming that opportunity or insight into a creative solution can get hung up in several spots.

People might miss the opportunity or insight when it occurs, or don't seek it out. They get comfortable with current success and their instinct is not to rock the boat if it's not a problem today. They may have been innovative in the past and want to take full advantage of that winning streak. Rather than thinking about the next opportunity, they get caught up preserving the advantage of their last solution. Think of the delayed use of the Internet in France. Most people there had a Minitel at home, a text-based system to get information and phone numbers, and to make reservations over a phone line. They continued to use Minitel instead of adopting the Internet as rapidly as people in other countries had.

If people are thinking about possibilities, another common first snag is when an idea doesn't make it out of a person's head. We have a tendency to self-censor—generating ideas is the responsibility of some other area, this idea isn't good enough to share, why bother because I won't get the resources, someone else must have thought of this already—so people don't articulate thousands of the ideas they have.

Some people toss around good ideas as potential solutions, but never work up the energy or excitement to take it any further. It may be that they have too much to do and not enough time for exploration. Perhaps taking an innovative approach to work isn't recognized or rewarded in their organization. Shifting priorities may make it seem a waste of time to put much effort into finding creative solutions. Think of the person who sees a wildly successful product advertised on television and mutters, "I thought of that three years ago!"

Some may be willing to try, but set their sights too low. They don't get enough support or they underestimate the necessary resources. They may give up too soon. They try once, fail, and then desert the effort as too hard, too costly, too complex, or some other "too." They mistakenly conclude that it's a poor idea, instead of realizing the flaw was in the environment. They set themselves up to fail, they do fail, and then they give up. Without perseverance, it's difficult to find a creative solution that works well. Just think if the Wright Brothers had given up their quest for flight after a few failed experiments—would aviation have progressed to today's level? Instead, they stayed at it, testing dozens of miniature wings at 45 different angles in a wind tunnel to find the shape that worked best. (Wright Brothers, 2005)

In other cases, people either overplay an early-stage idea or underplay it, and the idea dies young. Too much attention or structure can weigh down the quick tests and refinements needed when iterating. Too little attention, resources, or support, and the organization may squash it as a waste of time and people.

Some people take tiny baby steps, and they wind up confused and not making progress. Experiments need to be true tests. They need to be quick, rigorous, and clear, so you can understand what happened, what went well and what didn't, allowing you to quickly develop the next version. Good recordkeeping comes into play here.

Finally, some people pick a reasonable problem or opportunity to pursue, but then don't get the right people involved or they don't get the right people at the right stages. They may not have the idea generators, the experimenters, or the project managers to keep the project going. Without the right network of connections, their ideas may end up in a vacuum: *solutions looking for a problem.*

We'll get started by taking a closer look at how to recognize and select the right opportunities.

CHAPTER THREE

FIGURING OUT WHICH OPPORTUNITIES TO PURSUE

IN THIS CHAPTER

Going Prospecting ■ Identifying an Opportunity
That's Worth It ■ Framing the Opportunity

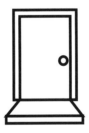

Where do opportunities come from? How do you know which are worth trying?

Getting focused on problems and opportunities is a critical first step in building creative solutions that actually will make a difference in how you, your people, and your company do business every day. Your or your team's creative inspiration may come as a result of the everyday problems or annoyances that you encounter. Many creative ideas are initially sparked by simple challenges in search of solutions.

The small, everyday problems that need solutions may seem too insignificant on the surface to warrant much of your time and energy. Many times they are small enough and have been around long enough that everyone has simply gotten accustomed to them. You may not even view them as problems, but as "just the way things are." Take a closer look, because you may find that by applying an innovative process approach, there could be great improvements in productivity, efficiency, or cost savings.

For instance, table saws have changed very little in the past 40 years or so, and, according to the Consumer Product Safety Commission, each year, more than 32,000 Americans are rushed to the hospital with table-saw related injuries, with more than 3,000 of those visits resulting in amputations. Stephen Gass, an amateur woodworker, had the idea that a safety stop could reduce the severity of injuries. He created SawStop, a triggering system that would shut down the whirring blade in 1/1,000th of a second when it came into the tiniest contact with a human finger. After building prototypes and testing with numerous hot dogs, he tested SawStop on himself—and it worked. He received a slight nick on his finger, rather than the amputation he might have received without the device. With this practical invention, he made table saws safer for other users. (Newsome, 2005)

"What I need is a list of specific unknown problems we will encounter."

www.CartoonStock.com

Although today's problems and challenges certainly may be worth putting some time and energy against, especially if the solution can easily create efficiency or save money, they are only one source of creative spark. There are many other sources that you need to tap into when determining the most important ideas to focus on. Manage in the present, but turn your attention toward future possibilities. What conditions do you anticipate arising, or can you create? If you only address the current and known problems, whether big or small, your solutions for the future will be underdeveloped.

GOING PROSPECTING

The reality of our typical workday is that we end up focusing the most time, energy, and resources on the most immediate, most visible, and most urgent demands. (Notice that these aren't the same as the most important.) That leaves precious little time to focus on the things that aren't as urgent or as visible, but that may be just as critical for future results. We need to pay attention to the obvious opportunities that present themselves each day, but we also need to look beyond them to reveal other sources of input. In other words, we need to go prospecting.

Employee and Customer Ideas

Those people who are most intimately connected with your business are frequently the best sources of creative spark. Customers (they can be internal or external) who use the product or service every day usually are the first to notice where there is room for improvement or enhancement. Your colleagues who have the most direct customer contact within the company, such as the help desk, customer service, or business development folks, are often the next in line to know what is not working as designed or what could be better.

By talking with or observing those people using the products or services, you can learn what features or options they wish were available or how they use workarounds to try and use a product in ways for which it wasn't originally designed. Research studies show that in many cases, it is the users who are the best source of creative ideas for a novel product, or for adapting an existing product in a new way. Think of all the creative ways in which you, as a user, modify tools, add an extra ingredient, or find a new way to do ordinary tasks more effectively. You are creating workaround solutions to everyday tasks that could be turned into creative solutions for others.

For example, a young inventor noticed the trouble his mother had while trying to transmit EKG data over the telephone to her physician using a standard pacemaker bracelet. Her wrists were too small to get a snug fit, so Brandon Whale had to press the electrode on the bracelet against her wrist. He set about improving the device, coming up with the PaceMate, an elasticized transmission bracelet using tiny sponge pieces soaked in an electrolytic solution to better conduct the EKG information. With this creative solution, he effectively improved the method that his mother and other patients used to transmit EKGs to hospitals. (Jones, 1998)

Customer Attitudes and Priorities

Even before clients or customers begin adapting and manipulating products and services on their own, their shifting attitudes and priorities are good indicators of developing trends and needs. Tap into these trends to identify potential areas for experimentation. For example, the Ford Edsel, now synonymous with product failure, made mistakes on multiple fronts in understanding customers' attitudes and priorities. Even though the car had many innovative features that are now standard, like an electronic hood release, they just weren't features that auto buyers were interested in at the time. Combine that with quality problems on the assembly line and the sticker shock of the first models to hit the showrooms, and it's no surprise that Edsel sales were dismal and its lifespan short.

A few years later, Ford did not make the same mistake twice. This time, rather than creating a car in search of a market, they discovered a market in search of a car. Their research showed that many families were looking for a second car that was sportier and more powerful than their main "family car," but that was still reasonably priced. They created the first Ford Mustang in 1964, catching the leading edge of the "muscle car" craze, with a list price of $2,500. Mustangs have continued to adapt and adjust as attitudes and priorities have changed through the years, so they continue to match the market. (Mello, 2002)

New Scientific and Business Knowledge

The significance and impact of new knowledge, in your own field or elsewhere, isn't always immediately apparent. It's through creative application and experimentation that knowledge and implementation ideas are coupled to develop practical solutions. Be a student. Learn as much as you can from thought leaders in a variety of disciplines and explore the potential connections between that new knowledge and your current business needs.

To illustrate this point, consider the adhesive Superglue, first discovered in 1951 but not connected to any immediate applications. A young chemist discovered the sticky substance when he was charged with finding a clear plastic that could be used to cast precision gun sights. He began working with a chemical compound that stuck to everything. Frustrated, he moved on, not thinking of applications for the sticky substance. Several years passed, and he was asked to work on finding an adhesive for jet plane canopies. A fortuitous mistake in the lab led to his team of scientists realizing they had a super sticky adhesive. It's now called Superglue.

Medics extended the usefulness of Superglue during the Vietnam War—they were trying to stop soldiers from bleeding out before they could get more thorough medical attention and they found that applying Superglue stopped bleeding and gave doctors more time to treat wounds. (Coover, 2000) Flash forward a few decades, and Superglue became a consumer product, used by anyone who needed a quick, strong bond between parts: model airplane builders, surgeons, homeowners, and others. At its start, it failed as a manufacturing plastic, yet the chemist didn't forget. He just needed another chance to find a use for the adhesive he'd created.

Systems and Processes

The various systems and processes that you use through the course of doing business can provide critical support for your efforts. They can help provide structure and efficiency to the things that you do on a regular basis, such as staffing, accounting, purchasing, and data analysis. On the other hand, their weaknesses can lead to delays, frustration, and inefficient workarounds. Even the systems and processes that work well today will likely need revamping or replacement as your work, industry, and needs change going forward. As a manager, your role is to both creatively use the existing systems and processes, and to architect new ones to meet future needs.

For example, a small electronics company was having trouble with its salesmen and, consequently, its customers. The salesmen were sloppy when entering orders and so some customers missed needed parts, or got charged the wrong amount of sales tax, or there was some other error. These errors made it difficult for the purchasing group to order raw materials, for the manufacturing group to fill the orders, and for accounting to bill correctly. So, the accounting department offered to help the salesmen, and to enter the orders into the system for them. Being more focused on details, the accountants noticed at the start of the process if a salesman had made mistakes or was missing data, and they corrected the orders. The result was happiness all around—the orders were correct, customers got their products right the first time, billing was easier, and the salesmen got proper commission for their work.

Emerging Technologies

Sometimes it's not a problem that is the source of a creative solution, but a solution that arrives in search of a problem to solve. New technologies, new methods, or new research may be just the missing piece to spark the development of a new way of doing something, perhaps for a problem that you don't even have yet. Creatively connecting emerging or underused technology in unique ways with practical applications is the real value of technology.

How would you run a computer, connected to the Internet, in a developing country? Electricity is generally not available in rural communities, or is erratic and expensive at best. But some humanitarians have seen around this problem and have persevered to bring computers (and increased educational opportunities) to some of the most secluded villages in the world. In 2000, the Solar Electric Light Fund (SELF), a nonprofit group based in Washington, persuaded Dell Computer and Infostat Telecommunications to donate comput-

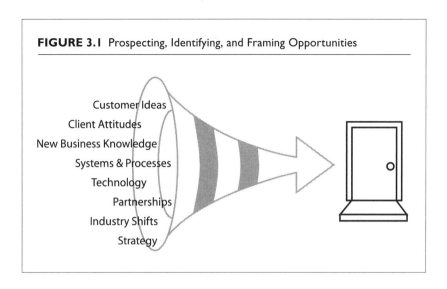

FIGURE 3.1 Prospecting, Identifying, and Framing Opportunities

ers and a satellite uplink to a remote rural school two hours outside of Durban, South Africa. Solar panels soak up the sun's power and provide the energy needed to run the computers. In just one year, the graduation rate for students rose from less than 30 percent to 70 percent. The benefits went beyond just the students; the isolated villagers found better ways of planting crops and marketing goods, which expanded their local economy. (Lipschultz, 2001)

As a manager, you may innovate at a local level, but some of those local solutions may have broader potential. Using solar power to provide energy to rural schools is one application. Using solar power more broadly in rural areas could account for $2.5 billion a year for solar manufacturers and enhanced economies and quality of life for the people living there.

Collaboration/Partnerships

Go beyond your own areas of expertise and the familiarity of your company's business. Collaborating or partnering with others can reveal unexpected opportunities for developing creative solutions. It's only when you interact more broadly with others that those potential connections will be revealed and perhaps evolve into real opportunities to work together in creatively developing solutions.

For example, a team needed to create a series of training courses that people would take on a computer. The team worried that the courses would be boring and no one would really finish them. One team member had a son who reviewed video games. The team spent an afternoon having him show them the most popular games on the market, and having him explain the psychological devices that video game makers used to "hook" players and keep them engaged. The team continued to consult with the reviewer, borrowing ideas from his area of expertise to make their learning programs more successful.

Industry and Market Shifts

Technology has made it easy for us to access all kinds of industry and market information about our customers, competition, and changes in the environment. *But what you do with this information, how you make sense of it and use it to drive your creative efforts, is what will set you and your company apart.*

Sometimes, a shift is broad enough to influence sweeping changes. The rise in child obesity is a critical health crisis in the United States and is seen as a collective problem that will require a co-ordinated effort across schools, families, industries, and government. For example, communities are demanding that schools implement nutritional standards in vending machines; parents are encouraging restaurants to offer healthy choices on the children's menus; advocacy groups are asking food, drink, and entertainment industries to voluntarily restrict advertising and marketing directed at children and youth, specifically for items such as candy, fast foods, and sugary cereals; and advocates are asking parents to do their part by making sure healthy foods are on hand at home and encouraging their kids to do more physical activity. Given this trend, the children's show Sesame Street shifted some of its focus in 2005, its 35th season on the air. Each episode now offers healthy tips on nutrition, exercise, hygiene, and rest. How is this affecting the resident Cookie Monster? He still loves chocolate chip cookies, but he also will be trying other healthy alternatives and he's learning that "a cookie is a sometimes food." (Carter, 2005) Sesame Street has picked up on childhood obesity as a problem, and has applied its creativity and reach in positive ways.

Strategy Realignment

The complex and dynamic nature of doing business today means that companies are constantly adapting and adjusting their business strategies as a result of a variety of forces at play—new technologies, globalization, converging industries, and a changing regulatory environment. Strategic realignment often means that, as a manager, you will need to extend your knowledge in new areas and develop new methods, techniques, and tools that allow you to do business in new ways. You have to get creative to adapt and solve evolving business problems.

Such a situation faced bank branch managers in 1999 when the U.S. Congress passed the Gramm-Leach-Bliley Act, which lifted many of the restrictions on banks. From 1933 to 1999, banks were limited strictly in what they could do; there was a strong separation between banking, insurance, and investment services. After 1999, though, banks could sell mutual funds, underwrite municipal bonds, offer insurance, give investment advice, and offer a whole range of financial services that they'd been prevented from providing before. Branch managers still needed to know about their traditional services—checking and savings accounts—but suddenly also needed to understand insurance policies, mortgages, and a range of investment instruments.

This new landscape became highly competitive. Middle managers in the banks and in their product and marketing areas had to learn about a fuller range of financial services, adjust their attitudes about stock markets, and start getting creative. They innovatively bundled services—one-stop shopping for credit cards, securities, mortgages, and checking accounts. They initiated customer loyalty programs, for example, targeting college students with low or no-cost accounts to get them in the door. These middle managers were at the forefront of a massive strategic change, and had to quickly figure out how to make it work. So much for a quiet, stable bank job.

IDENTIFYING AN OPPORTUNITY
THAT'S WORTH IT

As you probably now can see from all the potential areas you can tap into for creative spark, there are dozens of possibilities you *could* be focusing on. In fact, generating lots of potential opportunities usually isn't the problem. *Making decisions about what would be of most value and where to focus your time and energy is the more complex question.* How do you decide what's worth spending time on? What's worth investing the company's valuable, and perhaps scarce, people and resources in? Rather than taking on too many creative initiatives or initiatives that aren't aligned with the strategic results you want to create, *work on what is most important for the company and where you have the most leverage.*

One basic criterion is that the opportunity you want to explore further—the door that you choose to open—has a clear connection to the company's strategy and future goals. If it's not aligned with the general strategy, then it doesn't make any sense to put additional time and energy into pursuing the opportunity any further. In some cases, there is a major strategic shift in an element of your strategy and the new need is easily recognized and agreed to. A strategic shift may be a result of an environment change, such as new industry regulations or government policies. It may be due to market changes or new opportunities in certain geographies. It may be a response to a new technology whose impact is not yet fully understood.

In other cases, the strategic shifts are more subtle and more frequent, and you need to continually make sure that you understand where you're going and that the ideas you are exploring are still aligned with the most recent strategic adjustments. Change is a given, and you need to continually make sure that the results you envision and are working toward are still worth it.

Create an "A" list that defines the ideas where you have the most discretion and that would potentially have the most "bang" or benefit if you are able to discover some practical solutions. How valuable would those solutions be to the company? If the exploration of the ideas isn't feasible and the results aren't valuable, you shouldn't spend the time, energy, and money doing it.

A strong connection with your strategy and the possibility of really making a difference in the success of your organization or beyond is also what excites and engages others to join your efforts. If people don't feel like what you are working on is worthwhile and will make a difference, they won't fully commit to going along on an unknown journey of experimentation. Commitment requires them to find discretionary time in the margins to help with a project that isn't part of their regular responsibility. It requires them to reach out to their network and find ways to engage others to help in the process as well.

FRAMING THE OPPORTUNITY

Before you begin searching for ideas on how to approach the problem or opportunity you think is most important to focus on, stop to check that you have framed the issue in a way that really identifies the true nature of the opportunity. The challenges may be complex, and their solutions may not be clear-cut. Moving into "fix-it" mode too quickly may mean that you end up addressing the *symptoms* but not actually addressing the *underlying causes* of the problem. The symptom that is most visible today might go away, and another symptom related to the same underlying problem may then take its place.

The FOX television show "House" provides good (although fictional and quite dramatic) examples of how the process can work, as each week a team of doctors addresses only the cases that are the most baffling and difficult to diagnose. Patients present with a variety of complex symptoms (some related and some not), and it's up to the team to treat the most severe symptoms (i.e., keep people alive) while at the same time continuing to seek the real cause of the patient's trouble. In one episode, a patient presents with swollen hands covered in boils. The doctor suspects she reacted to soap because she was washing dishes when the symptoms first appeared. He gives her an antihistamine—treating the most obvious symptom, but not confirming first that this really was the underlying cause of the woman's boils. Moments later, the patient is gasping for breath, in the throes of an asthma attack. The doctor suspects an allergic reaction to the antihistamine. Eventually, they test her for all allergies. Yet, even in a "clean room" away from all potential allergens, she continues to show symptoms. They continue to explore root cause, going beyond what was first obvious, and discover that she was having a severe allergic reaction to copper, the result of a copper device implanted many years previously and a recent exposure to more copper—the pots she was washing. (TV.com, 2005)

You don't want to invest a lot of resources and energy only to discover down the road that you should have been looking at the situation in a different way or approaching the challenge from a different perspective. In your eagerness to find a solution, *avoid moving into choosing a solution too quickly.* Let's say your dining room ceiling is leaking. A bathroom is directly overhead, so you think it must be a leak from one of the fixtures. A plumber comes by, checks the toilet, sink, and shower—all are fine. You think, "Maybe it was a fluke; the plumber says it's OK, I've paid a big bill making sure it's OK—I'm done with the problem." But then, during a storm, the leak begins again. On more careful inspection, it seems that your rain gutters are clogged, and water is being forced under the roof and, you guessed it! That water is running down a wall stud and through a small hole in the ground floor ceiling.

Keep Asking Why

The paradox here is that you need to understand the problem deeply in order to seek and understand useful input, but not so much that you shut down to input. We each tend to frame problems based on our own experiences and solutions we've found that worked well in the past. We need to be more like the persistent child in the comic below who continues asking "Why?" than the adult who assumes she knows the answer. Instead of jumping to an answer, keep searching and asking questions to better understand the opportunity.

One way to gain a deeper understanding is to use the "Five Whys" problem-solving method that was made popular as part of the Toyota Production System (1970s). It was created as a simple approach that took any production problem and asked, "Why? What caused this problem?" The answer to the first why is usually an obvi-

© Batom, Inc. North America Syndicate

ous symptom that you might have predicted. The main point is to accept the answer, but to still ask why again and again as you peel away the layers to get to the root cause. Five is simply a nice guiding number. Complex problems often will mean asking why more than five times before you are able to gain greater insight.

A Simple Exploring Why Example

A large number of positions in a business unit whose success is critical to the company have remained vacant for a prolonged period, putting the business at risk.

Problem statement: Need to find a better way to quickly fill vacant positions with highly qualified people.

1. Why? Human Resources is taking too long with the candidate identification and screening process.
2. Why? HR can identify and line up a candidate slate pretty quickly; however, it is taking a long time to schedule and execute the interviews.

3. Why? The primary interviewers' travel schedules and work overload are causing a lot of reschedules and last minute cancellations. The number of candidates is also shrinking.
4. Why? Some candidates drop out due to frustration with reschedules and cancellations and some of the best people accept other offers while waiting. This means HR has to reinitiate the search.

At this point, you can start to see that the problem was originally framed as a human resources issue, which was a symptom but not the root cause. Targeting the business leader interviewers, their commitments, and their routines might have more effect in solving the dilemma. Of course, many of the challenges that you are working on may not be as straightforward as the example above. Complex business issues may require more than five why's and also may reveal that there is more than one cause at play. So, you could actually be working on a valid cause, and still not generate the results that you envisioned because you failed to address the other causes. These multiple causes are likely connected and intertwined, and your quest to find a viable solution may branch out in multiple directions.

Once you think you've discovered the root cause, stop and ask a basic question: "Does this cause explain everything I know about what the problem is and what it isn't?" If not, keep searching.

CHECKLIST

❑ Go prospecting across multiple sources to reveal interesting opportunities to develop creative solutions.
❑ Is the opportunity that you want to begin exploring actually worth it?
  • Does it connect to your company's strategy?
  • Will successful results make a real difference?
  • Is it both important and interesting enough to get people excited and engaged?
❑ Make sure that you really understand the opportunity before you move to solutions.
  • Continue to ask "Why?" and test your assumptions and beliefs.

CHAPTER FOUR

DISCOVERING OPTIONS AND INSIGHT

IN THIS CHAPTER

Engaging Others in the Process ■ Brainstorming: Generating
Ideas and Insight ■ Brainstorming: Leading the Process

ENGAGING OTHERS IN THE PROCESS

"We were young, but we had good advice and good ideas and lots of enthusiasm."
Bill Gates, founder of Microsoft Corporation

You've considered various everyday problems or opportunities you might want to work on. You've asked some questions and gained some clarity around the root cause of the problem or the details of the opportunity. Keep in mind, though, that the role of the manager is not to try and tackle these opportunities alone; rather it's to assemble the best talent and find solutions through others. It's time to invite others to join in the adventure, get them engaged and excited just as you are, and put your collective talents and resources to bear in thinking about how to approach the opportunity.

Be inviting, and tell a compelling story, because you don't have all the answers and you can't do it alone. You may be enthusiastic and ready to make things happen, but you're going to need help. You're not just looking for others to join in your efforts so that they can agree with your ideas and offer their resources to help your agenda. To build sustainable solutions, you need the diverse talents, skills, knowledge, and experience of a broader set of people—both within the organization and beyond its boundaries. Others can offer new information, new ideas, and new ways of thinking about the opportunity.

Each phase of the innovation process will rely on different strengths. Some people are really good at envisioning a future state and generating ideas of how to get there, others are best at seeing the big picture and the connecting relationships across all the pieces, and still others are most efficient at managing the details of large projects and implementing the big ideas of others. There is a strong reason why organizations have a diverse board of directors: Guiding an organization requires different types of expertise at different times.

The following example illustrates how the expertise and input of a larger interest group can address problems in innovative ways. In France, condominium law is similar to American law in that a homeowners association can impose late charges, put a lien on a condo unit, and force the sale of a unit when an owner doesn't pay monthly fees to the association. Instead of relying on a standard legal solution, such as a lien, one manager of a 465-unit condo in Paris developed a different way to handle the problem of late payments. He instead asked the condo association members for their help. When the group inquired about why the owner was unable to pay, they discovered that the owner had lost his job. The association loaned the money to the owner so that late fees would not be assessed and helped him find a new job, allowing him to pay back the loan and make future fee payments. By tapping in to all of the resources of the owners association, the individual owner's problem was solved, and they were able to avoid the trauma of legal wrangling and finding a new owner for the unit. (Keeva, 2004)

You want to build creative solutions that have a beneficial impact not just for your area but across the company. Each person brings to the table unique insights about the organization that, when shared, allow you to see connections through another lens. His functional area or division may be supporting the company's strategy in very different ways from your own group. He may have extensive experience in a particular division, product line, or geography of the company that can cast a different light on how you think about the challenge at hand, the root cause, or the potential solutions. He can help reveal potentially positive or negative impacts that you haven't anticipated.

You may have to be creative in finding ways to span boundaries and involve others. For example, the challenges of individual and small practice physicians are varied and complex, and also critical because they raise fundamental questions about the future of family medicine in the United States. Yet these doctors don't have a natural mechanism for interacting across their practices and sharing ideas. To better serve this widely dispersed population, the editors of *Family Practice Management* magazine challenged their readers to share their best ideas for solving practical challenges in their individual practices, problems that others were likely struggling with as well. One year later, they reported on 18 finalists who offered stories of resourcefulness and innovation: reducing overhead by removing anything not essential to the doctor-patient interaction; treating chronic illnesses with a team approach; implementing care alternatives for urgent patients; offering group prenatal care to extend the available education and support to patients; and merging independent family doctors and their staffs into a single medical group as a means of collectively approaching large problems that they were unable to solve individually. (AAFP, 2004)

Offer Them Challenge, Excitement, and Engagement in the Process

For all the people who join the effort, consider what most excites and engages them—then match the parts of your creative process to the people who are best suited or most excited by that part. Some of the fit and excitement will come from the unique talents that they have, part of it will come from the benefits of a solution that they envision. For example, for those most energized by the details of experimentation and implementation, the brainstorming or idea-generation sessions may elicit an audible groan. That's not what they most enjoy. However, once other people have filtered the ideas to one that the group would like to try, they're eager to join in and are an asset to the team.

We often have an image of inventors like Thomas Edison as working in solitude until that lightbulb of discovery suddenly lights up. In reality, Edison worked hard in a laboratory managed with few rules and filled with partners and associates whom he referred to as "the boys." Even if someone hadn't been invited to become one of the regular "boys," the door was always open for him to come in and use the lab for his own experiments as long as he paid for his own supplies and labor. The lab had talented collaborators who came and went frequently. The constant flow of people in and out had an added benefit of bringing many new perspectives on a problem. Outsiders were always welcome and they frequently offered a new approach to a stalled experiment. (McCormick, 2001)

Tap Their Collective IQ

Leverage your existing experience and the experience of others. There are many different ways of looking at a problem and figuring out how to approach it. Make sure that you are using all of the collective resources available to gain insight to the challenge that you've decided to work on. Don't just invite the regular or the obvious people to the table. People think and approach problems in different ways—use this to your advantage. At Duke CE, when we test a new learning method, we try to get a cross section of the company to act as participants, such as logistics people, computer programmers, executive administrators, project managers, Canadians, Brits, Americans, 20-somethings, and 40-somethings. By having different people with different perspectives and experiences, we can better see where our client's participants might have trouble with an exercise. We have a great group to brainstorm alternatives to the troubles, too.

Tap in to your social networks and intersections of communities. Each person involved in your project is also part of other networks within the company (their team, division, or geographic region) and beyond (professional organizations, social clubs, hobbies, previous employers, neighborhoods, etc.). Seek out and use those connections to make more connections. Start conversations with others.

Tell them stories of what you are working toward, what your vision is, and encourage others to tell stories as well. Invite people into your process, even if only for the length of a conversation.

Technology now allows interaction and collaboration across dispersed people in ways that were once impossible, and across multiple disciplines. Find ways to enable potential collaborators to easily interact. For example, uncommon illnesses can be difficult to understand and treat as a physician and difficult to manage day-to-day as an isolated patient who can't interact with other people who have the illness. Online support groups and communities of individuals who share health concerns and problems are now commonplace. Patients share their stories, explore ways to improve others' understanding of their illnesses, and sometimes provide insightful assistance to those treating them. Most of these patients would never have been able to "meet" and interact if things like dedicated Web sites, chat rooms, or discussion boards weren't designed for that specific purpose.

Similarly, some organizations set up team collaboration spaces—either physical space for them to spread out and write on the walls, or virtual space where they can share documents, ask questions, or schedule time to talk. This book series is an example of that, as the authors were rarely in the same place at the same time. Telecommunications technology allowed us to collaborate and create while being separated by as much as 14 time zones.

BRAINSTORMING
Generating Ideas and Insight

Brainstorming is a group approach to generating a large number of ideas in a short time, and is generally focused on a specific issue or challenge. It is probably the most widely used technique across multiple disciplines to stimulate creative thinking. If you've never participated in a brainstorming session, you're the exception rather than the rule. Most of us have been in many types of sessions that gather people and ask them to dig into and discover alternatives for addressing a particular opportunity. As a leader, you want to make sure that generating ideas and insight goes well—by both organizing the input of ideas and by facilitating the process—so that you get the output you need.

You want to begin with a clear statement of the problem or opportunity, but at the right level of specificity. You want something tangible, but not overly defined to the point that it will limit the generation of ideas and possible solutions. Don't enter this phase of the creative process assuming that *you* have the best idea, because it's very likely that you don't. Be prepared to challenge your assumptions, thought processes, views of the opportunity, and ideas about how to proceed.

Do others in the group view things differently? If so, spend time exploring their mental models and reframing the issues. If it's a new type of opportunity, you might explore and challenge your assumptions about your market, your customers, internal politics, or other constraints. If it's a problem, try redefining what the problem is *and* what it isn't to get closer to the underlying causes. It's sort of a process of elimination. Ask both "what is" and "what isn't" questions. For example, if a process breakdown is occurring, ask where it is happening and where it isn't, or what has changed and what hasn't. Don't ignore real data if it's available. What can data analysis tell you? You can turn data into an image or a picture, and a picture of what has happened often can provide a new insight.

Here are a few techniques for exploring an issue and potential solutions. Start by organizing what you know and then looking at it differently.

Find Analogies

Ask the group to consider how this challenge is similar to problems they've seen elsewhere. Whether bigger or smaller than the issue at hand, analogous problems or solutions in place elsewhere can offer insight to your challenge. For example, a neighborhood group upset with cars racing through their streets might find ideas by exploring how other types of "traffic, speed, intrusion, or barrier" issues are handled, and then exploring whether variations of those solutions would work for them. They might brainstorm a list of analogies and what they imply: strangers trespassing in your yard so you build a barrier or fence; ranchers controlling cattle with an obstacle gate that makes them go through in single file; boats navigating in a busy marina; athletes doing resistance training and slowing their motion down; building a bridge that has two decks—one for traffic and one for pedestrians; the body's immune system; etc. Not all analogies are useful on their face, but raising them may spark another idea.

Observe Others

Find the right people to observe—those who break the rules, take shortcuts, do things a little differently, or look at a problem from a different perspective. Although they think they're just doing something an easier way, they may hold a clue to a solution that also will work for you. For example, a couple in California took a unique approach to the issue of wild rabbits eating their lush garden. Rather than investing in expensive solutions designed to *remove the rabbits,* they simply accepted the interlopers but provided them with an alternate source of food. Every morning, they put out air-popped popcorn for the rabbits to eat. What could have been an adversarial relationship between human and rabbit became an enjoyable daily activity. The couple gets the pleasure of seeing cute little bunnies in their yard, the solution is inexpensive, and the rest of their garden remains untouched by the rabbits' sharp little teeth. (McFayden, 2005)

Use Appreciative Inquiry

Traditional problem-solving approaches focus on what's wrong and what's not working. Appreciative inquiry takes a different approach and focuses on both finding (inquiry) and acknowledging (appreciative) people's *stories of something at its best,* so that those qualities don't get lost in the improvement process. This approach assumes that in every group, whatever you want more of is already alive and well *somewhere* in the organization. Rather than focusing on problems and what doesn't work well, take a different view. Identify the best of what currently exists as a launching point to explore the possibilities of what could be.

As part of a senior project, Dan Lythcott-Haims, a product design student at Stanford, followed a wheelchair-bound student around campus for a few days. He discovered how awkward it was for her to take notes in class, because she had to sit a notebook on her lap and avoid the armrests on her chair. (The classrooms didn't have tables.) So, Lythcott-Haims began prototyping based on features he found and appreciated in similar solutions: auditorium desks that swung up from the side of the seat and airline trays that stored in the armrest. He preferred making a table with two sections that folded open like the airline trays did, because it would provide more working surface and store more neatly along the side of her chair. The designer incorporated the best aspects of similar products and then solved the problems that were unique to this application—thus discovering a creative solution to the student's everyday problem.

If exploring new market niches, ask if what you already do well could be used in other fields. For example, Canon's origins and expertise began in cameras and other optical instruments. They were good with lenses and pictures. They took that expertise in optical imaging and extended it into other fields, such as copy machines and video and movie recorders. Similarly, Corning parlayed their expertise in glass from cookware, to fiberglass, to other areas such as liquid crystal display and fiberoptics.

At a more operational level, if you are looking for ways to create a more effective team environment, ask people to think about what works well for them today (or has worked in the past) and share their stories as you consider how to apply those same techniques. For process improvements, find and acknowledge the areas where the process *does* work well; perhaps there is a technique or approach that will help in other parts of the process.

Change the Scope

Is the problem or issue too broad to generate good, feasible ideas? Are you getting bogged down in details or overwhelmed by the scope of the issue? You might consider redefining the larger issue into smaller, more manageable pieces that make the problem feel solvable.

For example, from its inception in 1980, MADD (Mothers Against Drunk Drivers) has grown from a small group of women in two states to the largest crime victims' assistance organization in the world with more than 3 million members and supporters. Their mission, "to stop drunk driving, support victims of this violent crime and prevent underage drinking'" is a large-scale one that they approach through a variety of smaller, organized efforts. Local chapters tackle public awareness in their communities; they organize a variety of projects, such as youth awareness programs and the most visible "Tie One On for Safety" red ribbon campaign during December. They also are responsible for popularizing the term "designated driver" to remind people to plan ahead for social events. MADD also works on removing drunk drivers from the roadways by pushing legislation in city and state governments. Their efforts and effects have been immeasurable in fighting this problem, and it's all been done through small projects that people did in their hometowns. (Lord, 2000)

BRAINSTORMING
Leading the Process

*"The best way to get a good idea is to get a **lot** of ideas."*
Linus Pauling, Scientist, Humanitarian, and Nobel Prize winner

It's important to consider the best way to approach brainstorming sessions and orchestrate them in a way that improves your likelihood of finding a variety of solid ideas. This means keeping people engaged in the creative process. University of Baylor management professor Blaine McCormick has described a classroom exercise in which he gives students 20 minutes to brainstorm at least 40 possible solutions to a problem. The students are then given a few minutes to identify their most promising ideas and present their *single* best idea to the rest of the class. One final assignment: They have to identify what number this idea was on their list of 40 or more. McCormick reports that the results are pretty predictable—the best idea usually numbers well into the 20s or 30s, and is sometimes a cross between an early idea and a late idea. The moral, he says, is not just to brainstorm, but to brainstorm for high numbers. (McCormick, 2001)

Getting the Ideas Out

- *Be clear on some basic criteria for your brainstorming session before it begins.* Keep the opportunity or problem parameters broad enough to generate lots of ideas, but not so broad that it turns into a session that is way off course.
- *Encourage everyone offering ideas to resist the urge to filter their thoughts before putting them in front of the group.* People have a tendency to self-censor or impose their own limitations; they consider sharing only ideas that fall within their definition of a "good idea." Set the example and put forward several wild ideas of your own. Are all ideas good? Not a chance, even though you may have heard the saying that "there's no such thing as a bad idea" in the past. However, even a bad idea can lead to a good idea if you continue to explore its attributes, so get all of those ideas out on the table.
- *Discourage people from making early comments, whether critical or endorsing.* There is plenty of time to debate later. Early criticism will stem the flow of ideas, as people are then wary of appearing foolish. Early endorsement also shuts people down when they think the best has already been found.
- *Don't settle for the first idea.* It's usually the most common solution and seldom the most creative. The more ideas, the better. Don't stop prematurely when you see one that looks good. Keep going. The best one is probably yet to come.
- *Try to build on or combine the ideas of others.* Look for connections, and combine two ideas into a better one.
- *Provide a way to capture all of the ideas.* It doesn't have to be fancy. Just make sure that ideas aren't lost in the mix when people start going quickly. Having them written down also lets others continue to review and consider them later on.
- *Don't let it go on too long.* Brainstorming can be tiring. Stop and let people consider the thoughts they've heard and toss ideas around in their heads. The best ideas may not come now, but later when they're in the shower or driving in the car. Give people a way to continue to pass along their ideas—e-mail, a discussion board, or perhaps another brainstorming session.

Exploring Them More

Once you have generated a number of ideas, it's time to take a closer look. One technique is to have each person select five top choices and then work only on those. An alternative approach that doesn't immediately eliminate any ideas and avoids focusing *only* on the bad or good points is the LCS method developed by some of the experts we work with in the field of innovation—Mitch Ditkoff and his colleagues at Idea Champions. This method asks each person to evaluate an idea by identifying:

- *Likes.* What she thinks are the best attributes of this idea
- *Concerns.* What gives her pause or makes her think it might not work
- *Suggestions.* How she thinks the idea could be even better

This is a good way to build from existing ideas, identify some underlying assumptions people have about the issue and possible solutions, and to generate ideas that more closely match the situation's specific needs.

CHECKLIST

- ❏ Who, beyond your own team, can you involve or entice into this idea-generation phase of the process?
- ❏ Have you looked at the problem or opportunity from multiple perspectives?
  - Creating analogies
  - Observing others
  - Using appreciative inquiry
  - Changing the scope
- ❏ Have you brought your assumptions out and then challenged them?
- ❏ Considering all factors, what approach will help generate the best ideas for addressing this particular opportunity? Will you use multiple approaches?

CHAPTER FIVE

FROM IDEAS TO EXPERIMENTS

IN THIS CHAPTER

Choosing the Best Idea ■ Enough Resources to
Get Started ■ Designing Experiments to Test
the Idea ■ Permission and Forgiveness

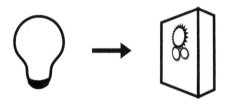

"I begin with an idea and then it becomes something else."
Pablo Picasso

It's often here, in the space between generating ideas and experimenting to solutions, that, for whatever reason, the process comes to a standstill. In your own experience, consider the number of times you've been a part of a group who generated ideas about how to do something, but the ideas never got off the ground. Sometimes, it's because the process has moved so slowly that people have lost the energy or excitement to take it any further. Sometimes, people have too many other responsibilities to spend any real time on the task, or they don't think their efforts will be recognized or rewarded. New priorities may make this idea seem like a waste of time now. Or, sometimes, it's because no one steps forward to be a champion and leader of the idea.

Once you and your group have become creative and generative, you need to take the lead in moving the idea forward. That's not to

say that you need to do all the work or make all of the decisions, because it's still a group effort; but ideas need champions and sponsors
if they are going to make it to the next stage.

There is some risk involved, but you have *good ideas* to choose
from and limited time, energy, and resources to put toward them. So,
you need to place some good bets and decide which ones to move
forward. Moving from ideas to real experiments is a big step and you
do need to make wise choices. You don't want to bring the process to
a standstill, you don't want to curb the group's momentum and enthusiasm, yet you do need to move forward responsibly.

Before going forward with this next phase in the process, you
should take time to reassess how well your best idea really addresses
the problem or opportunity, if you have sufficient resources to make
the experiments feasible, and that you have permission to keep
going.

CHOOSING THE BEST IDEA

You and your team have accomplished what you set out to do—
you've generated a lot of ideas on how to approach the opportunity.
Some are combinations or extensions of other ideas. What criteria
will you use to sort through them and select the best ideas? How will
the team select the most promising candidates for going forward? As
Figure 5.1 shows, you'll need a way to sift, filter, and combine those
ideas of all shapes and sizes down to one that the group agrees is the
best bet going forward, the one that creates the most excitement and
that people believe they can make work.

To test whether you are moving forward with the best idea, ask
yourself the following:

- *Does it fit the opportunity?* For those ideas that meet the core criteria, evaluate how well the ideas match the opportunity or address the real problem. Don't let the novelty and excitement of
  an idea obscure the fact that it doesn't truly address *this* opportunity. For instance, a start-up retailer of women's scarves,
  handbags, and other accessories sought to increase overall
  sales, because walk-in traffic to their one storefront wasn't gen-

FIGURE 5.1 Filtering Your Ideas and Insight

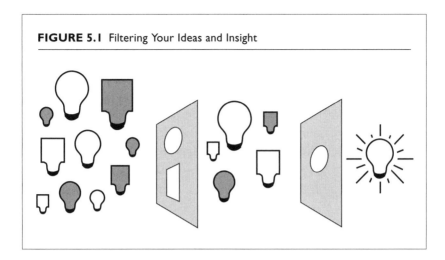

erating enough revenue. The owners were convinced they needed a Web site, so they turned to friends in the Web design field to create a site for them. The site was quickly developed and went live two months later. But sales didn't increase. Few customers used their online ordering system; instead, they called the store or came by. Although their site was attractive visually and had a lot of "zing," it didn't address the nitty-gritty of capturing a sale, because the online purchasing process was cumbersome and too time-consuming. Their big idea—a snazzy new Web site—didn't meet the mark. They failed to incorporate a key need—easy ordering—and so it missed the target of increased sales. With a revamp, they solved the problem by streamlining the ordering process, and were able to relaunch the site and increase their online sales.

- *Does it create value?* You need to understand the problem or opportunity well enough to evaluate if any solution you create is likely to be valuable; for instance, creating a vaccine for HIV would be valuable—it would solve a widespread health crisis. Creating a vaccine for bee stings would be less valuable; fewer people have severe reactions to bees and the market for the product would be considerably smaller, and thus, this product would be less valuable from both an outcome and a profit standpoint. Consider that in special circumstances when a pharmaceutical is seen as especially critical, such as the search for anti-AIDS drugs, the U.S. Food and Drug Administration (FDA) allows an abbreviated process for drug testing and approval called fast-tracking. The potential value is so great and the danger without a solution is so extreme that they are willing to truncate some of the normal processes.

- *Does it meet other criteria?* You might have any number of basic constraints, such as budget, resources, and time lines. Depending on the nature of the challenge, you may occasionally need to agree on these criteria *before* the brainstorming session in order to establish some general guidelines, but don't make the criteria so rigid that you stifle the creative process. If the problem was with the system for submitting travel expenses and billing them to specific projects, you might set guidelines, such as a solution should reduce the number of steps or people involved in any given transaction, it shouldn't increase the processing cost, and it should allow people who are out of the office to submit expenses.

As a manager, you need to think about doing a "back of the envelope," return-on-investment (ROI) calculation. This isn't a highly detailed analysis, rather you need to have a general idea of what a solution would cost and be worth. For example, would it save people time, generate income for the organization, reduce costs, or meet a larger societal need? If it's to generate income, then is it worth roughly $10,000 a year? One million dollars a year? Twenty million dollars a year? Think about what effect your innovation will have on others, and what benefits it might provide.

Finally, save those good ideas that don't make it through the core criteria or address this particular opportunity. Now may not be the right time, but as conditions change, they may become useful. Remember Superglue from Chapter 3. Your idea may not fit today but may prove of value in the future.

ENOUGH RESOURCES TO GET STARTED

Once you select an idea to place a bet on, you need to consider how to move forward with it. Do you have the minimum resources you need to get started with experimenting? If you can't tell a story that convinces a few critical people in the organization to give you the minimum resources that you need, then you may need to rethink if this is the right bet to place, or if there are other ways to begin your experimentation phase. This is a fine line; you need just enough to get started, but also some indication that you can get more later if needed. Don't set yourself up to fail—don't move ahead if there's not enough support to succeed at even small-scale trials.

You don't need to make formal requisitions and get permanent headcount at the start. In fact, you are better served to create temporary structures if you can. For example, a director wanted to create a product that was tangential to, but built off of, what the company normally did. It was a product extension that would result in new capabilities for the company. It had the CEO's full support. However, others in the company were not necessarily as supportive of this extension. The director and CEO created a temporary structure to support the effort and used another project as the guise for doing so; the CEO took a member of his staff and transferred her part-time to the director's team, ostensibly to meet the needs of that other project. The CEO then gave her remaining time to the director to use on the product extension work. Once the initial work on the product extension finished successfully, they were able to transfer the staffer permanently to the director's team. Had the project failed, the staff person would have returned full-time to the CEO's team.

Early on, it's often better to get resources informally. Borrow people's time in the margins—grab someone for a long lunch to get input, ask another to come by for an update that is so interesting he gives you three hours. Get a loan of equipment instead of buying your own. In that way, you can borrow and "steal" (time, especially) the resources you need, when you need them. However, you need to be aware that you use up social and political capital and goodwill when people lend you resources. As you are deciding where to place your bet, *ask yourself if this is a project that is worth spending your social capital on.*

Finally, keep in mind that it's successful experiments that will bring you more resources down the road, not your requests. Make the experiments count.

DESIGNING EXPERIMENTS TO TEST THE IDEA

"Here. Use this one, hon. I rigged it up so it'll
be easier on your back."

CLOSE TO HOME © 2003 John McPherson
Reprinted with permission of UNIVERSAL PRESS SYNDICATE. All Rights Reserved.

As you're designing experiments to test your ideas, keep in mind
that you're balancing tight time lines, limited resources, and the
need to make progress (and yes, failed experiments are progress). As
you iterate through your tests and make adjustments, design experiments that:

- *Are sensible but address key questions about the idea.* Design an experiment that tests the basic "will it work" questions, and also
  the "will it meet the core criteria" questions. In what areas are

you and your team least certain? What potential "show stop-pers" do you need to successfully address in order to keep going forward? Your initial experiments should be reasonable and help answer those questions. Consider a community group who wanted to construct their own building rather than con-tinuing to rent or borrow space elsewhere. Group members had two key concerns—whether they could actually raise enough funds to build a building and whether there would be enough use after the fact to support their investment. They decided to test their ideas with some key people: local (big money) donors, branches of the organization in other cities, and other organi-zations in the same city. They asked the donors about how likely they'd be to give money to the project, and what it would take to get their commitment. They asked the other organizations about long-term building upkeep, fundraising ideas, and how people use their buildings. They asked other local facilities about their operating budgets and usage statistics. Know what it is you hope to learn and be sure this experiment will give you at least some of the information you need.

- *Help tell you how to proceed in the next iteration.* Sequence your ex-periments so that each builds upon the previous one and helps provide more information about what changes to make or how to design the next iteration of the experiment. The results should help rule in or rule out potential changes. For example, think about an auto mechanic diagnosing a mechanical quirk. He runs tests starting with the most likely cause or the easiest to fix, then looks at other parts or systems if the initial tests don't reveal the problem. Each test gives him information about either something to repair or where to try next.

- *Give you some early indication of future needs.* Your experiments should also provide some indicators of future needs, helping you to anticipate what additional resources you will need in the weeks ahead, what other areas you might need to involve, or what partnerships might be helpful. Pay attention to these in-dicators as you plan. For instance, if a production process needs streamlining, do you have the people on your team who can make changes to procedures or equipment? Working with a computer programmer may help a marketing manager improve an existing ad-tracking product, but as they work through each iteration, they may realize that neither has experience preparing an applet for wide-scale use. To create a finished solution, they'll need additional resources.

PERMISSION AND FORGIVENESS

There is an old adage that says, "It is better to ask forgiveness than permission." We would say that when innovating in an organization, it is better to ask for both. The key is to remain proactive and seek permission to get the ball rolling, but not to let a lack of feedback be an impediment to your progress.

Ask for permission to move forward, to get some resources for your prototyping, and to ensure some political cover for what you are doing. Be "unofficially official." Have some support for what you're doing.

At the same time, given the rapid speed at which we work, it is impossible to ask for permission before you make every decision. You, as a manager, do have discretion and should be proactive. There may be parts of the project that are semi-public and some that you keep within your team. For example, people may know that you are working on a special project with another department but don't know the scope of it.

There are benefits to staying "under the radar," that is, keeping some of your experiment protected from public view. You actually place a bet with a project at several stages: when first deciding to move forward, as you're gathering resources, and after every round of experimenting. In the early stages it's often difficult to garner the level and type of support you need. In an otherwise busy day and hectic world, it's easier to say no than to really analyze and support something. You may find it beneficial to get some of the work underway, learn a bit more, and then be better able to demonstrate the benefits and challenges to others prior to unveiling the entire plan or project. A little "air cover" or shelter is sometimes needed while things are incubating. When you succeed, you can ask for forgiveness.

CHECKLIST

Before moving to experimentation, ask yourself:

- ❏ How well does this idea fit the opportunity?
- ❏ How well does the experiment fit the idea?
- ❏ What minimum resources do you need?
- ❏ Who else should you involve?
- ❏ Can you get political cover/support for now?

CHAPTER SIX

EXPERIMENTING TOWARD A SOLUTION

IN THIS CHAPTER

Implementation Is an Active Experiment ■
Piloting Your Solution ■ A Turning Point

IMPLEMENTATION IS AN ACTIVE EXPERIMENT

"The important thing is not being afraid to take a chance.
Remember, the greatest failure is to not try."
Debbi Fields, founder of Mrs. Fields Cookies

You and your enthusiastic team have selected what you think is the best idea, organized the critical resources, and decided to move forward with giving it a try. You are ready to begin the experimentation phase of the creative process. Is your idea likely to work as expected on the first try? Perhaps, but don't expect perfection right out of the gate. How many iterations will it take? Do you have the right or enough resources to build a solution that will work? These are unknowns, and there are no guarantees.

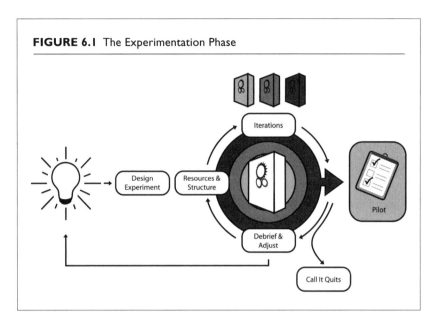

FIGURE 6.1 The Experimentation Phase

You may not know at the start, but you will learn more as you complete more iterations and experiments. Taking ideas to fruition may be harder than just thinking of them, but it's also more interesting. It's important for your team to begin this phase of the creative process with a collective view both of what you are trying to create and a realistic understanding about the nature of experimentation. Maintain the excitement and enthusiasm, and know that this is work.

As Figure 6.1 shows, during the experimentation phase you will need to

- design experiments that adequately test the idea,
- be prepared to complete multiple iterations of your experiment,
- debrief and adjust based on what you learn from each one,
- reassess the resources and structure that you need to keep moving forward,
- pilot viable iterations to learn more, and
- know if or when to call it quits.

Recognize the purpose and value of experimentation. As you get started, there are still a lot of unknowns, uncertainties, and incomplete information. You will be making a lot of decisions based on best guesses. It's through multiple experiments that you will learn more about the problem, what works and what doesn't. By analyzing the results, you can deepen your insight as to what the best solution will be and generate new approaches to try. Those tests that go well and those that don't are *equally* important in providing insight to the solution you are seeking.

For instance, Hollywood visual effects experts use a broad set of expertise—mechanics, kinetics, heat, electronics, chemistry, engineering, and mathematics—to create special effects. They often use a combination of methods to build, test, and adjust makeup, lighting, sounds, explosive power, locations of blasts, and so on when shooting a scene. In the movie *The X-Men*, effects experts needed to create the image of a train station's glass roof being blown apart, raining down on the people inside, and a lightning storm coming in through the shattered glass. They built a scale model of the set, adjusted the lighting, set the explosives, and filmed the result. They didn't like it. So, they spent several more months rebuilding the model, redesigning how to blow it up, and reshooting the scene. Reviewing the initial footage was critical. As in this case, if you don't get it right the first time, then try again and make adjustments until you do. (Singer, 2000)

Focus on Increments

Think back to the most challenging and rewarding accomplishment thus far in your work or personal life. If you had known just how complex or challenging it eventually would prove to be or all that would be involved, you might never have gotten started. When innovating, move forward in increments—simple experiments and small successes lead to bigger experiments and more success. Focus on the current step, the current experiment, the current deadline, rather than getting bogged down and overwhelmed by the total task.

The NASA Mars rovers took a long time to go from "Why don't we have a remote-controlled rover explore Mars?" to the first working prototypes that could handle varied terrain and avoid hazards, fit several types of sensors and analytic instruments on board, collect samples, communicate with its handlers back on Earth, and survive a crash landing on the surface. In the early stages of the project, one of the first challenges was to create a rover that could navigate the difficult Mars terrain while maneuvering around obstacles. If it were to become stuck, many of the mission's critical objectives would be impossible to achieve; therefore, the entire wheel design was critical. Engineers tried multiple rover designs using digital models on a simulated Mars surface before moving on to building the more expensive and time-consuming physical prototypes. Promising prototypes were then tested on a physical representation of the surface. An obstacle course nicknamed the "rock gauntlet" challenged the rover's wheels to scale everything from small rocks to concrete blocks to the deflated airbags that would be present after landing. By working in stages, the engineers were able to come up with a highly successful design for much less money than NASA traditionally spent on space vehicles. (NASA, 2003)

Adapt Structure and Resources

Understand that your needs will continue to change, and get creative in the ways that you fill the gaps between what you have and what you need. One of the most common reasons that people fail to innovate is that they don't realize that they have options in getting additional resources as they go forward. Consider whether you can span boundaries and shift or borrow some internal resources. Although there may be associated costs—you may have to repay the debt by letting others borrow members of your team later, or you may be asked to cover a portion of someone's salary—you understand them and are okay with that. Don't just assume that you are limited to your current resources without looking elsewhere.

Do what is necessary to ensure that the right mix of people is working on the problem, and don't assume that only a group of "experts" will do. Begin by being honest about strengths and weaknesses, your own included, and identify where you need to fill gaps. The resources that were helpful earlier in generating ideas may not be the best for designing and conducting experiments. Tap into people of diverse talents from various parts of the organization. As you cycle through multiple iterations of experiments, reassess what you need and know when to engage new people, new expertise, and new talents as the needs evolve.

In 1965, coaches of the University of Florida football team enlisted the help of physician Dr. Robert Cade, a kidney disease specialist, to help them understand why athletes lost so much weight and suffered from heat exhaustion during practices and games. Water, their logical choice, often caused stomach cramps and didn't really help the problem. The coaches understood the game and its athletes, but the physician better understood the human body. Intrigued by the problem, the doctor immediately approached colleagues and got them interested as well. They began by trying to figure out what was causing the physical symptoms. The athletes did their part by agreeing to participate in multiple experiments. Their research showed that all that sweat was taking with it the players' energy, strength, and endurance, and there were multiple causes. Electrolytes were out of balance, and blood sugar and total blood volume was low. The impact of all of these on the body was profound and could be deadly.

The answer, they thought, was to create a drink that would replenish what the athletes' bodies were losing during extended physical activity. But it tasted terrible. It was one of their wives who suggested the first flavor—some lemon juice to make it more palatable. Coaches evaluated the formula in real game situations and found that those who had the special drink mixture also did well on the field. Cade and his team had created Gatorade. Coaches, players, doctors, and an interested "friend" all contributed to this innovation. The formula has changed little over the years, and it's now being used by athletes around the world. (Kays and Phillips, 2003)

Get Comfortable with Failure, but Do It Intelligently

In the previous step, we talked about securing permission and forgiveness before moving forward to experimentation. That includes some level of forgiveness for failure, but along with that, an expectation that you will fail intelligently. The goal of each experiment should be to run it, find flaws, and fix it, not to find perfection or success in the first attempt. Understand that during experimentation, failure is likely but okay *as long as you can learn from your mistake.* Many of the problems you face are complex, and the concepts are novel. The key is to learn to fail intelligently. Fail in a way that allows you to understand why. Fail in a way that allows you to try again quickly. Use what you learn from failure and make the next experiment better.

Alberto Alessi is a third-generation leader of the Alessi company, famous for their creative designer kitchen utilities and tableware. One of the founding principles of the company was to work with leading designers to manufacture a variety of objects that would both fulfill day-to-day needs and be aesthetically pleasing. Alessi has been described as the *"godfather"* of Italian product design. He is known for walking the fine line between successful and risky projects, a line he describes in his own terms as the area between the *"possible and the not possible."* His advice for when you fail: Embrace your glorious failures, because that's where your insight and next big breakthrough will come from. As a testimony to their value, Alessi's product failures are displayed prominently in the company's private museum—in view of the design teams tossing around ideas for the next innovative product. (Wylie, 2001)

Throughout the years, some failures have actually been the birth of new disciplines of thought and discovery. The science of bridge aerodynamics was launched after the Tacoma Narrows Bridge, known to oscillate slightly in wind, collapsed in a moderate windstorm in 1940. The collapse brought quick recognition that engineers didn't understand and account for aerodynamic phenomena in suspension bridges in their designs. They needed new research to accurately predict these forces and then find ways to mitigate the danger they caused. The Tacoma disaster and its complex causes launched new studies of vibration, aerodynamics, wave phenomena, and harmonics in bridge design.

PILOTING YOUR SOLUTION

Think of piloting your solution as an extension of experimentation. Experiments are designed to test your idea, and pilots are designed to test your solution. After you've proved your idea through multiple cycles of experiments, and honed how to use the idea, you will get to a point that it's time to test the solution that you've designed—whether it's a product or a process—with others.

Because experimentation typically occurs in a controlled and simulated environment, there is no way to *really* know how the solution will work under "battle" conditions until you try it. Piloting adds a more authentic testing ground to the mix, complete with some of those people who may one day use this solution as part of their everyday work environment. Pilots help you learn more about people's habits, assumptions, and the conditions in which they operate, albeit at a smaller and safer scale. For more complex opportunities and solutions, you may run multiple pilots and return to experiment some more before you find the best version of your solution.

One manager describes a case where she thought that a solution had been fully tested and ready, but realized too late that the pilot environment and real use environment weren't quite the same: "We gathered a group of newly arrived executive students into a computer lab to complete an exercise with a new online library research tool. We had experimented with more than a dozen people internally and they were actively using the solution. What we hadn't accounted for was our classroom environment—we were suddenly asking 40+ people to press 'enter' at the same time. The search engine came to a screeching halt. We had to resort to asking each row of students to wait while the previous row entered their selection to finish the exercise. It was a painful learning experience, but now we understood the importance of considering *all* of the potential environments where a solution will be implemented."

Designing the Pilot

Selecting the best environment for your pilot is as important as the quality of the solution you've designed. Evaluate both *how* the solution will be piloted and *who* will be part of the process. The goal of the first pilot is to reveal any potential weaknesses in your solution, not to prevent them from being revealed. Consider what type of pilot will work best for a particular situation, keeping in mind that you want to design a pilot that will be tough, diagnostic, and fast.

- *Tough.* At the end of the pilot, you need to know definitively whether the solution failed or succeeded. You need to be realistic, but not risky. Resist an inclination to create a pilot environment that is so easy that it doesn't provide a real world evaluation. In the end, it doesn't serve you well and can create a false sense of security. On the other hand, be realistic and don't create a pilot that puts anything or anyone at risk. The pilot should be stringent enough to give you answers while you still have plenty of opportunity to make adjustments, but not so harsh that it puts your project, support, or resources in jeopardy.

- *Diagnostic.* What real data can you gather from the pilot that will tell you *why* you failed or succeeded? There may be multiple methods:

  - *Debrief and get feedback from users.* If it's a new process for doing something that you are working on, ask the pilot users to describe how work was going at various points throughout the process, and for their view of what happened when. For example, if you are piloting a new error-reporting system and all of the system failures were reported by people who used the system during a certain time period, you have narrowed down what to begin investigating.

  - *Gather real data.* If your pilot allows you to gather specific data, interpreting that data can help provide a more definitive assessment of the solution. For a new customer inquiry phone system, it might be the number of calls that didn't get through, the average wait time, the number of hang-ups, or the number of successful accesses on the first try.

- *Fast.* The pilot should let you know the outcome quickly. The goal is to design an experiment and evaluation that users can complete rapidly and at an opportune time for observation, data gathering, and analysis. It's important to consider what you plan to measure and how to do that efficiently. Having a small sample may allow for quick and detailed feedback; however, if only a few pilot users participate, your results may not be valid. Yet, having large pilots is more complex to arrange and to gather data. For example, if you plan to evaluate the pilot by asking users to fill out paper questionnaires, you will need additional resources to input and analyze the data. You might lose quite a bit of time translating data from one format

to another. Using an online questionnaire may solve this problem—the user enters answers to questions directly into the da-
tabase, and the analysis program can tabulate results within
seconds, rather than days. One group used an online survey to
poll attendees following a conference, and of the 250 people
polled, 70 percent responded, a significant statistical number.
Had the survey been mailed after the conference, requiring users to fill in and then physically mail back responses, the numbers would likely have been much lower, even in the single
digits.

Although an online questionnaire may not be the right way to
track data on your pilot, you do need to look at ways to capture data
efficiently and while the "iron is hot." Bottom line: You need to create a pilot where people participate in evaluating the solution
quickly and honestly, so you can move to your next step.

Nurturing the Idea

In the early stages of developing your idea or solution, it's important to nurture it along its path. Testing it too soon or too harshly
may abruptly put a stop to what may be the core of a really good idea
or solution. Consider an extreme example of "trial by fire," or testing something too soon and too harshly, in the way one ancient culture approached life.

The Spartan Empire was a short-lived one, with the Spartan culture based around athletics, sporting events, military training, and
physical superiority in battle. Life was made intentionally harsh for
the Spartan people, and each endurance test was thought to make
them tougher and more likely to conquer their enemies. Boys and
girls alike were bred to be tough, and began their tests of endurance
and strength from birth. Spartans took several steps to cull their population. As soon as a child was born in Sparta, the mother would
wash it with wine instead of water to make sure that it was strong—if
the baby was weak, it would die soon. It was then brought to a group
of elders who inspected the newborn carefully. If they thought the
infant was sick or obviously deformed, they (reportedly) tossed it

over a mountain cliff. Until around age seven, Spartan children were raised by their mothers, who taught them not to be fussy about their food, afraid of the dark or of being left alone, or prone to unpleasant whining. All of this was to encourage toughness and success as a soldier. Those who survived were the most physically fit.

A "Spartan" approach is a bit extreme and may needlessly remove some promising solutions. Your idea needs protection in its infancy or early stages. You are just beginning to explore the idea and discover all the possibilities. Later, you don't want a pilot that is so harsh it kills the idea in public. You want to provide protection and avoid the type of scrutiny that could bring the experiment to a premature halt.

Choosing the Pilot Group

Just as you need the right environment for running your pilot, selecting the right mix of people to participate is also important. You want to assemble an evaluation group who will:

- *Be sympathetic.* They are genuinely supportive of the idea and what you are trying to achieve, and they understand all the caveats of what it means to "pilot" something. They understand that they should expect the unexpected—that glitches are the norm for a first run. Their role is clear: to give it a whirl and see what happens, but to not expect perfection.
- *Provide honest feedback.* Being supportive doesn't mean that they will go easy in their assessment. They will provide genuine feedback—positive and negative—that is designed to help you understand where and how you need to do things differently in the next iteration.
- *Be opinion leaders.* They are supportive of the core goals and ideas and will be part of your extended network when they go back and spread the word about the potential solution with others. They have influence over others' opinions and potentially over the added resources you will need going forward. They also can provide guidance when it's time to move your efforts "above the radar" and into more public view.

A TURNING POINT

You've completed the first pilot of the solution you've designed. It may be something simple like a variation of an existing process that simplifies things for everyone. It may be a completely novel way of doing something that is very complex. In either case, completing the first pilot is a pivotal point at which you need to decide if and how to continue with the solution.

Understanding the Results

First, it's critical to take a step back and understand what happened. An "after action review" is a simple process that asks the following:

- What did we want to happen? What was our goal?
- What actually happened? What results did we get?
- Why did we get these results, both good and bad?
- What did we learn? What new connections and adjustments do we need going forward?

Recall the "asking why" approach that we introduced earlier. Return to the Five Why's here to delve more deeply into why you got the results that you did. As much as you design the pilot to simulate the real world, it's still just a limited instance. Remember, even if the results were as you'd hoped, you need to understand *why the solution worked in this pilot* in order to build a sustainable solution that can be implemented across the organization. There could be some unique characteristic of this pilot group that made it work, but that won't be present in all cases.

After completing your review, you have some decisions to make. If the solution still needs work, you may decide to keep experimenting or you may decide to call it quits.

Back to the Drawing Board

If the solution needs additional work:

- *Listen to your feedback, learn from the after action review, and return to experimentation.* Make any necessary adjustments to resources and methods. There is an old African Proverb: *Do not look where you fell, but where you slipped.* Similarly, your goal is to understand and learn from where the solution slipped.
- *Reassess what you need going forward.* You may make adjustments to the experiments, to your resources, or in which people are involved.
- *Return to the original idea, if needed.* Stick to your vision of the results you want to create, but be flexible in how that vision becomes realized. The idea may need to be combined with other ideas, or you may need to make a major adjustment in your approach.

Call It Quits

Be persistent enough to find out if you should continue, and then understand when it's time to stop. Decide when enough is enough and stop the experiments. Retain the ability and courage to end the project when you need to. For example, at one point in time, a major pharmaceutical company had a policy of rewarding the individuals on a drug-development team who halted a development project. It helped to counter people's natural tendency toward escalating commitment, even in the face of failure. (Blitt, 2002) Developing creative solutions requires commitment and excitement about the ideas you're exploring, but also the instincts that tell you when it's time to stop.

Implementing Solutions

If your solution has been successfully piloted, how will you develop a plan to extend the solution to a broader population? As with all other steps of the process that we've explored, consider what resources you need and who to involve.

Your goal is for it to integrate into people's normal way of working. Even for solutions that work, adoption is not always easy. There are multiple stories of products, processes, and systems that made it to this point, and yet failed when it came time to actually implement. Examples may come to mind from projects that have fizzled within your own organization. Even when the answer addresses the challenge and offers a sustainable solution, it still may challenge norms or ways of working. You need to be purposeful in implementation and move forward in increments.

Although various models have been developed to explain the typical adoption patterns of new ideas, practices, or products, most share reference to Rogers' bell-shaped Innovation Adoption Curve. This curve classifies adopters into categories and percentages based on the idea that some individuals are more open to change and adaptation than others. Thus, it makes more sense to begin with the easier (and smaller) segments, so that the merits of your new solution can gain acceptance and build momentum, rather than trying to quickly convert the masses. (Rogers, 1995)

It's important to consider the various subgroups to whom you will be introducing the solution. Each group adds credibility and serves as a growing reference base for the next. How you introduce the solution also is likely to vary for each group as you adjust for their interests and concerns. As we describe in our book *Influencing and Collaborating for Results,* you need to tailor your message and story for each group, and highlight how your solution benefits them.

CHECKLIST

❏ Have you prepared for multiple iterations of your experiment, and are you ready to adapt and adjust as you go?

❏ Have you designed a pilot that will enable you to learn more about the solution? Consider how you will address each of the following points:
  - Pilot group
  - Diagnostic/data gathering
  - Duration
  - Debrief and Adjustment

❏ Have you defined a stopping point for unsuccessful solutions?

❏ Have you planned how to implement successful solutions?

CHAPTER SEVEN

MAKING THE PROCESS WORK BETTER

IN THIS CHAPTER

The Dual Challenge of Managing and Sponsoring ■ Make Purposeful Changes ■ Making the Culture More Supportive

THE DUAL CHALLENGE OF MANAGING AND SPONSORING

To this point, we have talked about the process you go through to identify an opportunity and then create a new process, product, or service to meet it. We've talked about your role when you are actively involved in the process, and when you are leading others through it. You make sure the process is organized and the resources are in place to support it working well.

As a leader, though, you have a second role to play as a sponsor of other people's efforts. You need to help shape the environment for the longer term, and build a culture that supports inquiry, exploration and experimentation. Within your team, you help develop the mind-set, practices and routines that get people engaged and enable them to pursue opportunities that occur. The "way we work" has to include asking "what if . . . ?" You set the tone and model the behavior for your team as well as for others in the company. Wishing and advocating for a more creative and innovative culture is one thing; actually making it happen is another. Growing and embedding this approach into your culture so it becomes routine requires purposeful action on your part.

As we've seen in the previous chapters, discovering creative solutions is more than spontaneous creativity; it's a process, approach, and techniques applied with specific focus and outcomes. Harnessing the collective IQ of a group and turning good ideas into economically viable action requires a greater level of engagement, collaboration, networking, experimentation, smart risk taking, and willingness to learn from mistakes. These underlying behaviors, norms, and practices don't happen accidentally. To make these actions a part of everyday work life, you have to model and demonstrate what they look like and purposefully reshape certain organizational elements that may be inhibiting their development.

Leaders Who Emerge

One company that epitomizes the nurturing of creative solutions to everyday problems is W.L. Gore & Associates, founded by Bill Gore in 1958. The company's most famous product, Gore-Tex fabric, put them on the map. It can be found in clothing worn by hikers, skiers, astronauts, trekkers—anyone seeking waterproof, windproof yet breathable clothing. The company also applies its plastics product technology to industrial, electronic, and medical devices, and to health care products (Glide dental floss, for example). They are constantly searching for ways to keep applying that technology, regardless of how "out there" an idea seems.

What makes the company stand out is its corporate culture. There is little hierarchy and few "ranks" or titles. Teams are limited in size to promote clearer, direct communication and relationship building. There are no traditional "team bosses"—team members work for the good of the team, not for individual accomplishment. As one worker stated: "Your team is your boss, because you don't want to let them down. Everyone's your boss, and no one's your boss." This type of personal integrity allows employees to become "natural leaders" in situations—as individual credibility increases, more people are likely to want to work with you on your projects.

A case in point: Gore encourages its employees to work on speculative new ideas for about 10 percent of their time. One engineer, Dave Myers, was working on improving cables for mountain bikes. He successfully created better cables, allowing gears to shift more smoothly. Then, he applied this knowledge to other areas, such as animated puppet wires. He started tinkering with coating guitar wires—very small gauge wires—to test them for puppets. After coating them with a proprietary plastic, he thought the strings could actually be used in guitars. He then located a colleague, who was a guitarist, to help with the experiments. For two years, Myers and Chuck Hebestreit experimented without success. Another colleague at a different Gore plant heard about the effort and joined them. This third coworker, John Spencer, had just finished launching Glide dental floss. More people joined the "unofficial" project and, after three years of work, all of this "on the side" and without company oversight or asking for company permission, the team had something to present to the larger company and gain its support. The result? Elixir, a technological breakthrough in guitar strings, a product that hadn't been improved on in more than three decades. (Deutschman, 2004)

By encouraging its employees to collaborate and think creatively to solve problems, Gore allows anyone with an idea to lead an effort, gain support and resources, and build the future of the organization.

MAKE PURPOSEFUL CHANGES

"Act as if what you do will make a difference."
William James, American psychologist, philosopher, and author

As a manager you have greater leverage to create change than you might think. The fastest way to change the culture and behaviors of others is to start with you. Being deliberate in the areas that you have direct control over is your greatest source of leverage. There are four personal levers: modeling, routines, measures, and symbols. As you work each of these more purposefully, you'll see a change.

Model the Desired Behaviors

- *Get focused.* Connect your work to strategic priorities. Understand the issues and how your group plays a key role in the company's strategy. Select a few important issues to focus on and make meaningful connections for people; help them understand why their work is valuable and requires creative solutions. For example, if cost cutting is a priority, can your team improve their processes to reduce inventory on hand, or speed up accounts receivables coming in, or increase the number of calls per person, etc.?
- *Be a student.* Build a network of intelligence and awareness beyond what you know well. Sometimes managers can become so specialized that their exposure to outside information, knowledge, and ideas also becomes limited. Talk to those outside your field. Take courses in new technologies or approaches. Have diverse interests. Encourage and enable others to spend time outside the organization as well: they might study how others are solving similar challenges and how your industry or environment is changing, and anticipate the need for future solutions.
- *Span boundaries.* Learn more about issues across the organization and how they are affecting others beyond your area of responsibility. Advocate and enable people to share resources and support across boundaries. Don't resist ad hoc behavior or

temporary structures as people work on ideas and experiments. Work to build your network and relationships.

- *Remain open to input* even though you may know the problem deeply. Recognize that your knowledge alone isn't enough to solve the complex challenges you face. Be willing to search for new ideas, theories, or approaches through each phase of the process. Recognize the value of maintaining time to reflect, time to free associate, or time to meet with staff just to chat about whatever they're thinking about.

Set Routines

Routines help direct people's attention and effort. What you ask about, check up on, plan, or discuss sends important signals and guides your people's actions. It's important to do the following:

- *Set aside time and resources for innovative efforts.* Whether it's meeting to generate ideas or experiment, having dedicated time allows people to devote their full attention, more so than sporadically catching a minute here or there. Even when we recognize many of the challenges are important, they often fall prey to the "tyranny of the urgent."
- *Establish short-term deliverables or action items.* Milestones and deadlines, even if self-imposed, have a way of keeping people engaged and giving more substance to a project.
- *Take routine breaks to recharge the spirit.* Many of the challenges you face will prove particularly difficult. Solutions will not be easy. Ideas may be slow in coming, it may take many more iterations than you expected, and pilots may have disappointing outcomes. Take breaks to renew and re-create the spirit and enthusiasm with which you began.

Measure, Recognize, and Reward

Simply put, if it's not important, don't measure it. If it *is* important, take care that you do. People pay attention to what gets measured. It means someone is watching and cares.

- *Measure doesn't equate to counting.* As Albert Einstein is quoted as saying, *"Not everything that counts can be counted, and not everything that can be counted counts."* Changes in the culture and approach to developing solutions will be subtle over time. They can't and shouldn't necessarily be "counted" but are visible, noticeable, and demonstrate measurable progress.
- *Note and reinforce innovative shifts in others.* As you model the behaviors you want others to emulate, take time to let them know when you notice them incorporating those behaviors in their everyday work. Let people know that you notice and encourage their efforts to be more open to input during discussions, to make connections and learn from others across the organization, and to be a student of the industry.
- *Accept and learn from failure, but don't measure it.* Expect and accept failure on first attempts, and protect your people from any negative repercussions. Avoid individual accountability and finger-pointing when you don't get the results you'd hoped for in the experimentation phase. Instead, focus on learning and problem solving. Think back to our earlier examples of perseverance—Edison, the Wright Brothers, T.S. Eliot. What might have happened if measures of their attempts and failures had been allowed to deter them?

Symbols

What you draw attention to can reinforce or deter your efforts. Be aware of the significance that you give, because it will be noticed and modeled by others.

- *Recognize diverse efforts and contributions.* Each phase of the process builds on what came before, and the contributions at each phase are critical. The people who can put clarity around the core challenge, those who are good at generating ideas, those who have a knack for putting ideas together in a unique way to address the challenge, and those problem solvers who work the idea through iterations of experiments are all valuable contributors. Recognize all contributions along the way.

- *Celebrate the milestones.* When you or your team members reach a goal, think about the implications and note the progress you've made, especially how much closer you now are to a solution. Some challenges will be more complex and it will take longer to design solutions. Don't wait for the "big" success to celebrate. Celebrating progress along the way keeps people engaged and signals that what you're working on is important.
- *Don't point the finger of blame.* Not all bets, even intelligent ones, will come through. Just as you celebrate success collectively, acknowledge failures as a team, and move on.

MAKING THE CULTURE MORE SUPPORTIVE

Another component of your job in leading the process is to identify and align portions of the key organizational processes, structures, and policies that may be inhibiting an innovative approach. Your vision is to actively engage the group and get the best results for the organization, but it will take time to get others committed.

Keep in mind that your ideas may challenge established assumptions and ways of doing things. Everything about the current environment—culture, systems, processes, and people—has been created over time and aligned for a different purpose. Your efforts may challenge this environment with new ideas and new ways of working.

You're not going to change it overnight, and you can't tackle too many issues simultaneously. Don't attempt to change the world all at once. Be smart and do what you can do. Identify the high leverage areas, the areas where moderate effort will have good return. Iterate.

The organizational capabilities and characteristics that can help or hinder your efforts to build an innovative culture span a range of elements.

❑ *People.* Your ability to achieve results depends on your ability to engage a variety of people with a diverse set of knowledge and talents at each phase of the process. This involves both engaging the people you have today, and building and attracting new talent in the future.
  • Are you focused on matching the interests and aspirations of your own team to the opportunities you address?
  • Do you have a compelling story to tell them?
  • Is the organization being deliberate about attracting people who embrace an innovative and creative approach to finding solutions?

❑ *Environment.* What kind of environment would most support your efforts? What culture, feeling, relationships between people, and partnerships are needed, available, or missing?
  • Are intelligent risk taking and experimentation encouraged?
  • Does the organizational structure enable or prohibit people from collaborating beyond their own team?

❑ *Systems and processes.* What operating procedures, standards, work methods, or infrastructure are helping or hindering your efforts? What do you need to build for the future? For example, do recognition and rewards systems reinforce innovative efforts, and not just the "big ideas" or high-profile products?

Finally, as you experience some success in implementing creative and innovative processes, building sustainable solutions, and developing a culture that supports this new approach, you also should build a reputation for sharing the credit. Over the entire process of creating anything of real value, there are many people who will have contributed in a variety of ways.

Many will be visible and directly on the front lines, but many more will be hidden behind the scenes. Some will be active within the core team, others will help indirectly by providing flexible resources, such as access to meeting space, or by introducing you to others who could help. All will be valuable to the process. Recognize and include everyone in your successes. The more you release credit, the easier it will be to gain more resources and support and to make people want to work with you again.

Those who really matter will know and recognize the real value of your contributions.

BIBLIOGRAPHY

American Academy of Family Physicians. 2004. "Big Ideas to Help Your Practice Thrive." *Family Practice Management* 11 (8): 27–34. http://www.aafp.org/fpm/20040900/27bigi.html. (Accessed July, 2005.)

Ante, Spencer E. 2003. "IBM," *Business Week* 3859 (November 2003): 84.

Bellis, Mary. 2005. "Liquid Paper." About.com. http://inventors .about.com/library/inventors/blliquid_paper.htm. (Accessed July, 2005.)

Bergstein, Brian. "Timecard Lets Workers Punch in from Outside." *The News & Observer* (Raleigh, NC) 19 June 2005.

Blitt, Barry. 2002. "Fresh Start 2002: Weird Ideas That Work." *Fast-Company* 54 (January): 68.

Carter, Chelsea J. 2005. "'Me Eat Less Cookies,' Says Cookie Monster." The Associated Press. MSNBC.com. http://msnbc.msn .com/id/7421924/. 8 April 2005.

Coover, Harry W. 2000. "Discovery of Superglue Shows Power of Pursuing the Unexplained." *Research Technology Management* 43 (5): 36.

Deutschman, Alan. 2004. "The Fabric of Creativity." *FastCompany* 89 (December): 54.

Drucker, Peter F. 1985. "The Discipline of Innovation." *Harvard Business Review.* MA: Harvard Business School Publishing. Reprint August 1, 2002: 1–7.

Hannoosh, Dr., James. 2005. "History: Background on the Invention." http://www.raising-canes.com/html/history.html. (Accessed June, 2005.)

Healey, Jon. 2004. "Following Pepsi's Lead, Coke Tunes In to Net Music Scene." *Los Angeles Times.* Los Angeles, CA: 29 January. C.1.

Hickam, Homer H. Jr. 1998. *The Rocket Boys.* NY: Dell Publishing.

Houghton Mifflin Co. 2005. "Cotton Gin." *The Reader's Companion to American History.* http://college.hmco.com/history/readers comp/rcah/html/ah_021100_cottongin.htm.

Howell, Jane M. 2005. "The Right Stuff: Identifying and Developing Effective Champions of Innovation." *Academy of Management Executive* 19 (2): 108–119.

Jones, Diana Nelson. 1998. "8-Year-Old Boy Wins Accolades for his Invention," *Pittsburgh Post-Gazette,* 21 September 1998.

Kanter, Rosabeth Moss. 1982. "The Middle Manager as Innovator." *Harvard Business Review.* MA: Harvard Business School Publishing. Reprint July 1, 2004: 1–13.

Kays, Joe and Arline Phillips-Han. 2003. "Gatorade: The Idea That Launched an Industry." *Explore Magazine* 8 (1). University of Florida Research and Graduate Programs. http://rgp.ufl.edu/ publications/explore/v08n1/gatorade.html.

Keeva, Steven. 2004. "Lose the Box," *ABA Journal.* 90 (9): 84.

Kelley, Tom with Jonathan Littman. 2001. *The Art of Innovation.* New York: A Currency Book, published by Doubleday.

Levitt, Theodore. 1963. "Creativity Is Not Enough." *Harvard Business Review.* MA: Harvard Business School Publishing. Reprint August 1, 2002: 1–9.

Lipschultz, David. 2001. "Solar Power Is Reaching Where Wires Can't," *New York Times,* 9 September 2001. http://www.self.org/ news/NYTimesArticle.htm. (Accessed July 2005.)

Lord, Janice. 2000. "Really MADD: Looking Back at 20 Years." *Driven Magazine* (Spring).

MacLeod, Donald. 2005. "How the Waste Land Was Done." *Guardian Unlimited.* http://education.guardian.co.uk/higher/research /story/0,9865,1511326,00.html. (Accessed July 15, 2005.)

Manning Innovation Awards. 2004. "Safety Turtle® Helps Protect Toddlers from Drowning Accidents," Calgary, AB: September 13. http://www.manningawards.ca/pressroom/2004f.htm.

McCormick, Blaine. 2001. *At Work with Thomas Edison: 10 Business Lessons from America's Greatest Innovator.* Canada: Entrepreneur Press.

McFayden, Joni. 2005. "Creative Solutions for Gardens' Pests," *Letters, Los Angeles Times,* 5 May 2005, F8.

McWilliams, Peter. 1994. *Life 101.* Prelude Press.

Mello, Sheila. 2002. *Customer-centric Product Definition: The Key to Great Product Development.* Boston, MA: AMACOM.

Nalebuff, Barry and Ian Ayres. 2003. *Why Not? How to Use Everyday Ingenuity to Solve Problems Big and Small.* Boston, MA: Harvard Business School Publishing.

NASA Jet Propulsion Laboratory. 2003. "Wheels in the Sky." *Mars Exploration Rover Mission.* May 30, 2003. http://marsrovers.jpl.nasa.gov/spotlight/wheels01.html. (Accessed July, 2005).

Newsome, Melba. 2005. "He Came. He Sawed. He Took on the Whole Power Tool Industry." *Inc. Magazine* 27 (7) 87.

O'Connor, Kevin with Paul B. Brown. 2003. *The Map of Innovation: Creating Something Out of Nothing.* New York, NY: Crown Business.

Pearson, Andrall E. 1988. "Tough-Minded Ways to Get Innovative." *Harvard Business Review.* MA: Harvard Business School Publishing. Reprint August 1, 2002: 1–8.

Phillips, Frances. 2005. "Inventor gaining notoriety." *The Daily Tribune News* (Cartersville, Georgia), 4 April 2005.

Pinchot, Gifford and Ron Pellman. 1999. *Intrapreneuring in Action: A Handbook for Business Innovation.* San Francisco, CA: Berrett-Koehler Publishers, Inc.

Rogers, Everett. 1995. *Diffusion of Innovations.* 4th Ed. New York: The Free Press.

Ryan, Thomas J. 2004. "It Is Essential to Stay Creative Amid Big-Business Bureaucracy," *Apparel* 46 (3): 5.

Schwartz, Evan I. 2004. *Juice: The Creative Fuel That Drives World-Class Investors.* Harvard Business School Publishing.

Singer, Bryan, dir. 2000. "The Special Effects of the X-Men." Disc 2. *X-Men* 1.5 Edition. DVD. Twentieth Century Fox Home Video.

Thurrott, Paul. 2003. "MSN in Major Industry Shift." *WindowsITPro.* 17 March 2003. http://www.windowsitpro.com/Articley/Article ID/38366/38366.html?Ad=1

TV.Com. 2005. "Damned If You Do." *House.* Episode 5. Originally aired 14 December 2004 on Fox.

UPS.com. 2005. "Amazon.com to Thank Customers with Surprise Special Deliveries by Their Favorite Stars." http://pressroom.ups .com/landing/0,2111,25,00.html. (Accessed July, 2005.)

Von Oech, Roger. 1998. *A Whack on the Side of the Head,* Third Edition. New York: Warner Books, Inc.

Wright Brothers Aeroplane Company. 2005. "Through a Tunnel." http://www.first-to-fly.org/History/Wright%20Story/tunnel .htm. (Accessed July 15, 2005.)

Wylie, Ian. 2001. "Failure Is Glorius." *FastCompany* 51 (October): 35. http://www.fastcompany.com/magazine/51/alessi.html.

INDEX